Grassroots Spirituality

Praise for *Grassroots Spirituality*

"Grassroots Spirituality" is an amazing document. Reading it was like an intravenous infusion of encouragement about what is taking place "out there." . . . it is richly deserving of a broad audience." Larry Dossey, MD, author of *Rediscovering the Soul,* and *Healing Words.*

"This is a seminal book. It describes the emerging phenomenon of the kind of spirituality many of us have been individually exploring without realizing the extent to which society has been experiencing it. This work has to get out!" Martin Rutte, co-author, *Chicken Soup for the Soul at Work.*

"Robert Forman . . . offers an outstanding and impressive report which reveals a surprising and pervasive theological agreement within the Spirituality Movement. His exciting survey graphically illustrates the possibility of this movement shaping a creative era where an unwavering current of spirituality ignites sustained meaning and responds to new and old needs of religiosity." Angeles Arrien, Ph.D., Cultural anthropologist; author of the *Four-Fold Way* and *Signs of Life.*

"This is an important document about a profound shift in the nature of spirituality in America, and could presage a major 21st Century trend." Philip Goldberg, author of *Roadsigns on the Spiritual Path.*

"Robert Forman is in a unique position to inform us about grassroots spirituality. For the past several years he has been conducting both informal and formal research with participants in this movement. He brings to this task his background as a scholar of religion and a faculty member, with the analytical tools to assess, analyze and communicate to us about the significant features of spirituality in the United States today." Harvey Aronson, Ph.D., Director Dawn Mountain Tibetan Temple.

"My major comment is: Wow! Hooray! Just what the world is waiting for!" Felicia McKnight, Director, Si Belle Retreat Center.

"*Grassroots Spirituality* is an incredible piece of work! Well thought out and well written, it covers an amorphous topic with great intellectual ambition and integration. Dr. Forman is the perfect person to do this. He was able to see current phenomena in the context of history and world religions." Rachel Harris, Ph.D., Eselen, author of *A Child Learns What They Live.*

Grassroots Spirituality

What it is
Why it is here
Where it is going

Robert K.C. Forman PhD

with a contribution by
Kathryn Davison PhD

IMPRINT ACADEMIC

Copyright © Robert K.C. Forman, 2004

The moral rights of the author have been asserted
No part of any contribution may be reproduced in any form
without permission, except for the quotation of brief passages
in criticism and discussion.

Published in the UK by Imprint Academic
PO Box 200, Exeter EX5 5YX, UK

Published in the USA by Imprint Academic
Philosophy Documentation Center
PO Box 7147, Charlottesville, VA 22906-7147, USA

ISBN 0 907845 681

A CIP catalogue record for this book is available from the
British Library and US Library of Congress

Contents

Why It Is Here

Where It Is Going

Chapter I

*Introduction**

> *Quietly, irrevocably, something enormous has
> happened to Western man. His outlook on life
> and the world has changed so radically that in
> the perspective of history the twentieth century
> is likely to rank with the fourth century, which
> witnessed the triumph of Christianity, and the
> seventeenth, which signaled the dawn of mod-
> ern science — as one of the very few that have
> instigated genuinely new epochs in human
> thought. in this change, which is still in process,
> we of the current generation are playing a cru-
> cial but as yet not widely recognized part.*
>
> Huston Smith

Subtly, unmistakably, and irreversibly, our civilization
is undergoing an astounding shift. Our whole outlook
on life, our understanding of the world and the infinite,
the way we connect to one another and to the world are all
changing profoundly. So profoundly that many people
feel that our age may come to be known the "second axial
age," where the future of world civilization diverges so
sharply from what has been that nothing will remain unaf-
fected.[1]

This world shift touches on many things: how we relate
to each other, how we work and do business, how we gov-

---

* This Forge Institute research project was supported
by a very generous Grant from the Fetzer Institute.

ern ourselves, how we spend our free time, how we heal and how we die. Many of these changes center on the development of a fundamentally new form of spirituality—focused on the personal, experiential and transcendental. This new form of spirituality is being developed not by some solitary religious seer or within some shadowy monastic cells. Instead, unlike any previous religious revolution, it is being developed by a huge, far reaching yet largely disorganized body of ordinary people all over the world, and especially in North America. It is populist, so far disorganized and enormous, as we will see. We call this the Grassroots Spirituality Movement.

Though many have observed the recent fascination with spirituality, the depth and significance of this movement is not widely noted. Neither the size, breadth nor importance of what is going on has been generally grasped. This is typical: journalists of the 1950s were, at best, dimly cognizant of what was going on in black church basements all over the South. Even when the first marches began, few recognized the enormity of the social and political changes—led by Martin Luther King, Rosa Parks, Nelson Mandela, Fanny Lou Harner and Raymond Abernathy—then afoot.[2]

Yet the growth of spirituality may be of even greater significance than was that civil rights movement. For its shudders may potentially impact every corner and subculture of our civilization.

Signs of this buzzing, disconnected eruption of Grassroots Spirituality are everywhere:

- Between a third and a half of Americans believe that they have had a spiritual experience that has had a significant impact on their lives.[3]

- 23% of U.S. Citizens say they regularly do yoga, meditation or other stress reducing exercises.[4]

- 59% of Americans in 2001 described themselves as both religious and spiritual while 20% view themselves as solely spiritual. Of those, 80% say that spirituality influences every aspect of their lives, while only 42% of those describing themselves as religious describe it as central to their lives.[5]

- Roughly 40% who call themselves religious are not members of any particular church, mosque or synagogue.[6]

- 12% have had a personal experience of a great spiritual figure — God, Jesus, Mary, Elijah or Buddha — has appeared to them. This equates to 22 million Americans who feel that they have had some direct contact with the ultimate.[7]

- 41% of Americans have experienced something they describe as miraculous, a physical or emotional healing, or a healing of a broken relationship or the like.[8]

- 1,158,850 people are registered members of the spiritually- oriented Alcoholics Anonymous. It is estimated that more than 5 million souls are currently active in some 12 step group—ALANON, overeaters anonymous, sexaholics anonymous, and so on.[9]

- There are approximately three million active small spiritual groups in America, according to Robert Wuthnow. Approximately 70 million Americans, some 40%, are currently involved in one or more of them. Another 8 million have been involved within the past three years. (These figures do not include all the children's and teenagers' groups.) If this number were spread out evenly over the country, in a typical town of 50,000, there would be at least 600 small groups; in a city of two million, 25,000![10]

- Over the past two decades many of the non-fiction books that have remained the longest on the New York

Times Bestseller list — *The Road Less Traveled, Care of the Soul, Chicken Soup for the Soul* — are about spirituality. Their sales have reached millions. When American newsweeklies put something about spirituality on the cover, their newsstand sales have gone up substantially.[11]

Though as we will see participants in this movement are found in great numbers within many traditional churches and synagogues, this spiritual movement is burgeoning mostly on the margins of mainstream, popular culture and traditional church hierarchies. It is growing not in science labs, parish naves or university classrooms, but rather in living rooms, church basements, Yoga centers, nature walks, meditation rooms and coffee shops all over the nation and world. It is at heart populist, devoid of leadership or overarching organization. And it has the potential to change the face of American society and our planet's civilization.

Dissatisfied with narrow, dogmatic religious views, and frustrated with strictly rationalistic worldviews and life goals, this new Grassroots Spirituality Movement is attempting to integrate consciousness, soul, and spirit into our societal dialogues. Slowly it is weaving these into our understandings of the nature and purpose of life and reality, into our workday and family lives, into our global politics, and into our future.

From the perspective of centuries, a sea change of this breadth and magnitude may be unstoppable. But, as Huston Smith notes, we of the present generation have a choice. If we are among those who feel that this new kind of spirituality is worth fostering, we can aid its growth and speed its maturation. Or we can just sit on our hands and let this potentially valuable cultural movement continue to develop in a disorganized and amorphous way for decades or centuries.

If we work intelligently, thoughtfully and in concert, we whose lives are shaped by and dedicated to these new principles enjoy an enormous and exciting opportunity to nurture, enhance and channel this burgeoning wave and help bring our culture to greater and more profound peace. Though Grassroots Spirituality is unquestionably lively already, we may be able to enhance and help guide its growth, and help it soak into the channels and rivulets of our society. We cannot cause the changes that are afoot. But we can help them mature.

If we don't do our jobs well, we will have lost an incredible opportunity to infuse our civilization with these more spiritual and open minded values. If we do live up to the challenge of supporting, legitimating and enhancing this phenomenon, we have the opportunity to sculpt and give birth to a new, holistic and far more deeply humane way to think, see and live. It can be one element of our learning to live together on our small, small planet.

The choice is ours.

Notes — Chapter I

[1]   Ewert Cousins, *Christ of the Twenty First Century* (Rockport, Mass: Element Books, 1996), p. 9.

[2]   Cf. Norman Lear, The Search for E Pluribus Unum, speech to the National Press Club, Dec. 9, 1993.

[3]   Gallup Pole, *Emerging Trends*, Vol. 19, #7, Sept. 1997, p. 3; Princeton Survey Research Associates, 1994. See also David Hay, *Religious Experience Today: Studying the Facts* (Lon: Mowbray, 1990), p. 79

[4]   Hart and Teeter Research companies for NBC News/ Wall Street Journal, June 1996; quoted in Duane Elgin, Global Consciousness Change: Indicators of an Emerging Paradigm, p. 15. This is confirmed by a study by Barna, 1994. See George Barna, *The Index of Leading Spiritual Indicators* (Dallas: Word, 1996), p. 63.

[5]   Spirituality and Health, Spring 2001, as reported in *Religion Watch, March 2001.* Poll done by Blum and Weprin.

[6]   Egon Mayer, ed, The American Religious Identification Survey, 2001, reported in USA Today, Monday Dec. 24, 2001, 1D.

[7]   "The Epidemiology of Spirituality," a report given by George Gallup, Jr., at the Spirituality and Healing in Medicine II Conference, Harvard Medical School, 1996, p. 3.

[8]   Ibid, p. 2.

[9]   Alcoholics Anonymous Pamphlet, 1997.

[10]   Robert Wuthnow, *Sharing the Journey* (NY: Free Press, 1994), pp. 46, 48, 55.

[11]   According to T. George Harris, publisher of *Psychology Today*, presentation to *Fetzer Institute*, Sept. 1997.

Chapter II

Anthropologists in La La Land

There are many more of us out there than any of us really know. What is happening in the world, in my view, is that there is a new spiritual awareness. We are in the consensus building process about who we are as human beings, who we are as spiritual beings.

James Redfield[1]

How Big Is Grassroots Spirituality?

Sociologists have known for years that there is a deep split down the middle of the American religious psyche. While survey after survey has found that some 94 percent of us believe in "God or an infinite spirit," there is a deep divergence within our society about what that broad phrase means.

One large group of Americans understands God in the traditional way: "a personal God." He or She is something like a person, who judges us for our actions now or at the end of our lives and to Whom we might pray for help or support. The other group seems to hold something much less coherent. For most of this group, the ultimate reality is not personal but more like a "universal energy or spirit," which somehow connects us with the greater reality or

Grassroots Spirituality

energy behind the world. A spark of that universal energy "indwells" within us.

It is that second group, those that hold to some kind of a universal energy or infinite spirit that we will be studying in this book. This is not to say that the more traditional group is not interesting, vast or important, or that their views are not valid. But that group has its own students, and its sociologists are legion. We are looking here solely at the other, less studied, less recognized path. This book may be one of the very first to do so.

Now, just what is the size of our Grassroots Spirituality Movement? No fewer than six independent surveys suggest something of the size here.

1. The Barna Research Group found that roughly 1 of every 5 Americans, or roughly 20%, are what they call "new age practitioners." These, they say, are the people who hold that faith is a private matter, that the ultimate is intermingled with the self and who are focused more on religious consciousness than ritual practice.[2]

2. This number is quite near to the 1997 study by Zinnbauer et al. They found that 19% of their sample viewed themselves as "spiritual" but not religious.[3]

Barna's and Zinnbauer's fifth of America, or roughly 52 million people, becomes the low end of our estimate. But theirs may be too exclusive of a definition. Both leave out the more or less institutionally affiliated souls who may hold to an "intermingled ultimate" and perhaps hold some other spiritual attitudes, but attend a religious institution and/or do not identify themselves as New Age.

3. Perhaps we should take as the *sine qua non* of this movement those who hold to a view of God as non-personal. In a recent Gallup survey of American beliefs, it was again found that 95% of the respondents were believers in God or an ultimate spirit. The interesting fact however was that of that, only 66% held to a "personal God."[4] Some 34% (that's of the 95% and thus some 32.3% of the total

population) espoused a non-personal God, something closer to an "ultimate spirit."

This number is quite close to a second finding of Barna's. He found that 28% of Americans define God in spiritual terms.[5]

Let's think about these numbers. It is well known that people generally give pollsters the more "socially accepted" viewpoint. "Personal God," we know, is the traditional or "acceptable" view. Most good Catholics, Protestants or Jews were taught about a "personal God" in their parochial, Hebrew or Sunday schools classes. They were taught that "God loves us," "He will watch over us" and that they should pray to God for He will answer their prayers. That between 28% and 34% gave some anonymous telephone interviewer this *un*conventional, socially *dis*approved answer is little short of amazing, is it not? For it means that people are rethinking these theological conventions enough to *volunteer* the "unacceptable" answers to a stranger.

4. While Robert Fuller finds that almost 40 percent of Americans have no religious connection, only about half these, or 21% of all Americans, are what he calls "spiritual but not religious."[6]

5. Wade Clark Roof finds that somewhere between 9 and 19 percent of the total US adult population is what he calls "highly active seekers, or people for whom spiritual and metaphysical concerns are a driving force."[7] Roof's numbers may mark the low end of this movement's size, for this excludes those who frame their spirituality in more ecological terms, those for whom seeking is real but not "a *driving* force" and those who attend church or synagogue and are also actively seeking.

6. Given our sense that some members of this amorphous movement may be within a tradition, perhaps we should define the movement in terms of a more complex set of spiritual attitudes, not just a theology. In 1995 Paul Ray identified 5 general complexes of religious attitudes.

His types 4 (an engagement with spiritual experiences and an emphasis on personal growth and the religiously mysterious) and 5 (an emphasis on personal spiritual growth along with seeing nature as sacred) seem to get at key aspects of this Grassroots Movement. Ray found that some 31.7% of the population holds to these views.[8, 9]

It is important to note that Michael Hout and Claude Fisher recently found that the number of people who told pollsters in the General Social Survey, taken by the National Opinion Research Center, that they have "no religious preference" rose from about 7 percent in 1990 to about 14% by 2000. This, they found, does not indicate a lessening of religious or spiritual sensibilities, but rather a falling away from the mainline traditions. While this is not quite the same group as the grassroots spirituality group we're looking at here, their finding is not unrelated. [10] See below.

In sum, our estimate is that between 19 and 32% of Americans hold to a more spiritual, non-personal God view of the ultimate and/or a new-age-like sympathy with spiritual processes. This translates to between 49.6 and 83.2 million souls. While data for the rest of the world is scantier, we believe something like this percentage can be found in every major industrialized nation as well.

However, these numbers leave out another enormous sub group: the people who *do* identify with a religious tradition, but remain open minded, exploring a range of traditions, tools and paths. These people combine traditional religious views yet remain sympathetic to spiritual processes and religious mysteries. These people, according to Paul Ray, comprise *an additional* 26.8% of the population. Their attitudes *include* an open minded interest in the spiritual, but they retain their church or synagogue going patterns and much of their language. Their beliefs and attitudes are highly various.

Combining these two groups, people who are open-mindedly interested in the spiritual may be as large as

58.8% of Americans, or 152.8 million Americans! If this is correct, then interest in spirituality dwarfs Judaism, Islam, and every single denomination of Christianity! Finally, it starts to become clear why so many of the best selling non-fiction books are about spirituality! The Grassroots Spiritual Movement may be the biggest movement to come onto the religious/spiritual scene since the reformation.

"But wait a minute!" you might say. "Aren't these numbers much too high? After all, isn't America always said to be the 'most religious' of the industrialized nations?"

Sure. As any scholar of the current American religious scene will tell you, Gallup and other telephone surveys have shown that, year after year after year, attendance at churches has held to a remarkably steady and high 40%. Though some denominations have increased, Protestants claim their overall numbers have not significantly changed since the 1940s. Though one wonders about the long-term future of this scandal ridden institution, Catholics say their numbers have been stable since the 1960s.

So when we see such huge numbers of people interested in a new form of spirituality, it just doesn't seem to add up. (Or rather it adds up to too much!) How can *all* these people attend church so regularly, yet at the same time be exploring "new spiritualities?"

First of all, there is no conflict here. Many people go to church services and also quietly explore a variety of spiritual views alone, with friends, and in small groups. They pray to Jesus and read Rumi and D.T. Suzuki. (See Chapter 6)

Secondly, recent findings suggest that these traditions' numbers may be substantially inflated. In an important study, Kirk Hadaway, Penny Marler and Mark Chaves wondered about the accuracy of these renowned steady attendance figures.[11] To check them, they conducted an *actual* head count across an Ohio county, and then compared it to the pollsters' claims about attendance. They

found that indeed, while roughly 40% of people *told* telephone pollsters that they attended church within the past
week, only *about half* that number *actually* went. According
to their more accurate count, *only 19.6%* of their Ohio
Protestant sample and, at most, *only 28%* of Catholics actually showed up at church in a typical week. "Protestant
and Catholic Church attendance," they found, "is roughly
one-half the levels reported by Gallup."[12] That's roughly
20%.

Why this a discrepancy? As we mentioned earlier, people are often unwilling to tell telephone pollsters, strangers, what they might consider socially unacceptable.
"People like to see themselves (or present themselves) as
'better' than they are, based on a traditionally accepted
social or moral norm."[13] (This is not uncommon: 16% of
non-voters, by one recent count, tell pollsters that they
voted.[14]) Perhaps, they also speculated, white collar workers, evening shift employees and childless folk may have
been out of their houses at dinnertime when the pollsters
called, and thus weren't counted. Whatever the reason,
while many Americans *verbally* identify themselves as
faithful church goers, only about half that number actually
are. The churches may have a less of a grip on the American religious psyche than they claim.

This trend is underscored by the findings of Michael
Hout and Claude Fisher: folks that believe in an ultimate
but have "no religious preference" doubled in the past
decade.[15]

Spiritual Discrimination

In 1992, Dr. Colin Greer, the director of the New World
Foundation, asked us to research the spirituality community. He asked us to find out who was doing what, who
was bringing spiritual folks together, and whether it was
all as new-agey and irresponsible as the press was por-
traying. "I think," he said, "that a lot of people are

involved in spirituality, but are embarrassed to talk about it at the office or to their friends."

Ray's, Barna's, Zinnbauer's and Gallup's findings all confirm Dr. Greer's suspicion about the size of the spirituality movement. His second thought was right too. That summer I traveled around the country, interviewing men and women about spirituality. Virtually every one of them told me that despite the fact that they had been involved in spirituality their whole adult lives, they were very slow to tell people, or to use that term in the workplace.

Why? Just think about the words that the press — to many of us — have used to refer to people involved in spirituality: "the New Age", "hippy dippy," "flakes," "weirdocs," "cultish," "spirituality fad," "airy fairy," "kooks," "woo woo," and, my personal favorite, "in la la land." If someone were to say in their office or a cocktail party that he or she was into "spirituality," they would be instantly labeled "weirdo," they told me, and strangers would back away from them.

Around that time I worked as a computer consultant at a major eastern bank. After I had worked there many months, Madeline, a thoughtful, thirty-something middle manager, invited me to lunch. She took me to a busy restaurant quite far from the office. Only there, she said, many blocks from the bank, was she willing to confide in me that she had practiced meditation and had been involved with Muktananda's Satsang. She felt she would "never move up if anyone knew."

There's a word for fearing for your job because of your involvement in your choice of a spiritual or religious group. *Discrimination.*

When you cannot tell anyone of your interest in spiritual growth for fear of being denied the next advancement, that is discrimination. When you can share your books on new ways of growth only in secret with people you know you can trust, as Madeline did, that is a quiet form of *oppression.* When you cannot share your most life

changing mystical experiences with your minister because
he or she will look at you as if you are crazy, that is a form
of *prejudice*. When your newspaper, your office mates, or
your golf partners unthinkingly label your interest in spirituality as "flaky" or "weird," this is verbal bigotry. While
still the First Lady, Hillary Clinton imagined that she was
speaking with Eleanor Roosevelt; she was pilloried by the
press as either cultish, crazy, or both. This is *intolerance*.
Just think what we would have said had she invited a
Rabbi into her office to lead her in a prayer exercise. Yes ...
nothing. When every leader of a new religious group is
instantly branded as the next Jim Jones or David Koresh,
this is guilt by association, bigotry by another name.

Over the last decade, this embarrassment seems to have
lessened. People seem to be more willing to admit to their
spiritual interests. Buddhism in the late 90s became chic.
Spirituality has now found its way into a few corporate
and government offices, as we will see in Chapter 6. Some
health care agencies seem to be opening to the possibility
that spirituality might be of value. During our interviews,
many told us they are still slow to speak of their work in
professional settings, but my impression is they were not
as adamant about this as they were years before.

There are lots of reasons for this discrimination. I don't
want to go into them in detail, but some of them are no
doubt well-deserved. A very great number of unverifiable
claims have been made under the name of spirituality: the
claims of crystal wearers, aroma therapists, channelers,
and "Heaven's Gate" members have made many cringe
(or even worse: laugh!). Many leaders of spiritual groups
— notably Jim Jones, Rajneesh, Trogyam Trungpa
Rimpoche, and Zen abbot Richard Baker Roshi — have
been accused of sexual and financial abuses.

But some of this discrimination may have more insidious causes. For example, church leaders may discriminate
because they feel threatened: If any lay person can reach
"Christ Consciousness" through intensive prayer or con-

templation, what happens to the priest's role as mediator? Does a populist, open minded movement threaten the church hierarchy? If a mystic can have an insight directly from the spirit, what happens to the unchallenged authority of the Bible or of the priest?

Corporations too, and the media that earns its living solely from their advertising dollars, may also have a subtle though probably unconscious interest in keeping spirituality down. If all you or I need to find satisfaction is a quiet place to sit, or a wooded path to walk, then what use do we have we for ever-new shirts, skirts or skee-doos? Spiritual people tend to live more simply. If a large number of people begin to simplify their lives and slow down their pace, then what will happen to the Christmas rush? Corporations have a vested interest in putting spirituality down.

Yes, there are many unrecognized social forces that may be tending to discourage spirituality through discrimination or ridicule.

Such discrimination has an unnoticed effect. It keeps the interest in matters spiritual — an interest so enormous that, we've seen, it dwarfs Judaism, Islam, and every single denomination of Christianity — largely hidden and marginalized. Unable to talk about their interests openly, many read their spiritual books largely in private, still keep secret the retreats they attend, and meditate generally alone. Spread out, the spiritual movement lacks a center, a large scale community, or even a name. And people who are exploring their spiritual lives in a range of ways have no natural ways to meet or support each other's quest.

All this makes a huge difference. Think of the difference between the woman who reads Deepak Chopra in the privacy of her bedroom, or attends a weekend with him once or twice, and her friend down the road who goes to a church. The church-goer "knows" that she is part of a huge community, the so called "body of Christ," which includes church members all over the nation and world. She has a huge community that reinforces her beliefs and commitments. She sees people around her who think roughly as she does, and thus "confirm" that her path is, on the whole, OK. She "knows", because all her church mates largely agree, roughly what is true and generally acceptable in her community. She knows where or how to find other like-minded souls, even when she moves to a new town, and roughly what they will believe. And she knows that if there is a task to do, like fight discrimination against her people or fight abortion rights, she will be able to count on the help of thousands of people across the nation. Even if she never taps it in any way, merely by being part of a larger church structure, she carries the emotional and intellectual reassurance that her cohesive community provides.

Down the street, her spiritual friend reads Deepak's books alone, in the comfort of her bedroom. If she feels that she has learned something enormous from Chopra, she may tell one or two friends with whom she shares her interest. But she has no larger community with whom she can share her excitement. There is no natural way for her to find like minded people to talk about such matters, for there are no church basements in which to post a note. If she feels that she wants to correct a social wrong, or if she experiences discrimination, hers will be a largely lonely voice in the wilderness. For she is without a support system.

In effect, the oppression that the society has (unconsciously?) foisted against the spiritual has tended to make its "members" lonely, confused, and largely disenfranchised. Being marginalized does this.

Why This Study?

In 1997 we were given a generous grant by the Fetzer Institute to research and describe the range and extent of the broad Grassroots Spirituality Movement — Buddhists, Neo- advaitan meditators, Esoteric Christians, Renewal Jews, Taoists, spiritual healers, the spirituality in business consultants, and so on. They asked us to map out the beliefs and practices of this far reaching community. We have continued our research through 2002. As we've seen we didn't need to revisit the question of its size. Ours was not a quantitative study. It was qualitative. We were curious about the range and pattern of its general beliefs and practices, if any. We wondered if it was as flaky as the press has made out. We wanted to hear the voices of this thoughtful, disorganized but stigmatized world, and map out its geography. We also wondered why it had appeared in the latter half of the twentieth century and where it might be headed.

Here were our questions then as we began our interviews with diverse spiritual teachers, leaders and participants.

• Is there a single group here in any sense?

Are the views we would hear coherent enough that these people could even begin to talk? Do its members share enough of a world view that they might be able to even communicate? Secondly, could we help its members come together and communicate? Our implicit suspicion was that the viewpoints and languages would be so different that these disparate folk might not be able to talk comfortably with each other. After all think how little some Muslims can talk to some Christians.

• How might the spirituality movement best develop better relationships?

If we could find ways to help these folks interact productively, what might we do to help them develop interrelationships? In other words, how might we help integrate the larger cross-traditional community of spiritual seekers?

• What are the causes of this enormous movement?

This then is why we began this study. We wanted to hear the voices, understand the ranges of opinions, tools and mechanisms of this movement, so that we might determine if this loose gaggle of seekers could communicate or develop into something like a community across the great religious divides. Perhaps we might find new ways to help truly bridge the ancient religious chasms that have so troubled humanity's history. If someone could indeed help bring together this enormous but fractured movement, what might they all do together? What are its new values and ways of interacting? How might they be applied to society, to the workplace, to our educational system, and to our lives? What in other words might spiritual people do to help the larger world?

Anthropologists in La La Land

Imagine yourself as an anthropologist entering a new and sometimes strange tribe. You know it's a huge tribe, but you don't know quite what its members believe or think. Let's call our tribe La La Landers. You wonder what they're really like.

Well, how does an anthropologist find out how a new culture thinks or discovers the range of its beliefs? Well the first step is generally to talk with them, to hear their voices, to listen to their stories. If to this tribe spirituality is not about a "personal God" or about "salvation from sin by ritual sacrament," then what *is* it about? What *do* people in your diverse community actually believe about the ultimate? What *are* their attitudes? What *do* they do to contact the infinite?

These are complex matters. Survey data like Gallup's or Ray's don't begin to address these more nuanced questions, for you cannot readily tease out people's deepest beliefs and feelings by neatly bubbling them into a "God" "Universal Spirit" or "Other" category. Quickie telephone surveys, for all their value, just cannot tell us what these non-traditional people actually hold, or are doing in the privacy of their living souls.

For example, Gallup found that 32.3% of their respondents believe that there is a "universal spirit?" Well, just what is a "universal spirit" to them? Is it like the Native American view of a universal interconnected multiplicity of spirits in the mountains and rivers? Is it monism, the understanding that all is one thing and that the world is illusory? Is this universal spirit like a person? Like an energy? Or is it closer to a belief that nature itself is holy? How are the things of the world related to that "universal spirit?" Are they part of it? Separate from it? Separate but related somehow? Does all of this 32.3% think about it similarly?

And just how should human beings make contact with such a universal spirit? Do they talk about meditation, quiet prayer or movement techniques like Tai Chi key? Do people primarily use guided imagery? Do these La La Landers think we should talk about spirit in a special way? Are words irrelevant? And how do spiritual people talk of this "universal spirit" in their workplaces, churches, healthcare, government offices, and what have you? So from surveys we know that this movement is huge, but we don't know quite what its beliefs, practices and doctrines might be.

When anthropologists discover a new tribe, how do they learn about its members' range of beliefs and general directions of thought? The time-honored way is to turn to what is known as the "anthropological technique," "key informant" or "strategic informant" technique. The anthropologist chooses people who are, by virtue of their position in society, their knowledge, or their personality in a particularly key position to inform us about the new tribe. The anthropologist might talk to the chief, the medicine men, the housewife everyone confides in, or to some particularly astute soul who has developed an unusually encompassing view. He or she would seek out anyone who might substantially add to their understanding.

To understand the tribe's beliefs and general directions, anthropologists don't seek out a strictly *representative* sample of the culture. Knowledge is not distributed proportionally to every group or individual. It is unevenly distributed. Some informants are — by position, personality or talent — better able than others to teach. Of course, the anthropologist also knows that to get a complete view, those informants should come from or have a clear understanding of the range of the important sub-cultures within their tribe.

How might an anthropologist choose the key informants in our La La Land? There are untold thousands of "key" people who teach meditation, lead spirituality groups, run Tai Chi centers, organize Christian spirituality retreats, bring spirituality to the hospitals, teach Jewish mysticism, and so on. Obviously we could not speak with every trustworthy informant who might have a clear view of this enormous tribe. Completeness is clearly impossible! So what one would do is to seek out a large number of strategically placed informants.

We interviewed 92 in the first round.* We sought out people who could add to our total picture of this tribe, both by virtue of their position within the world and also by virtue of their reputation as potentially helpful observers of this scene. Since beginning this research, we at The Forge Institute have continued to have deep and long conversations with several hundred more "key informants." Our observations about the beliefs and shape of the Grassroots Spirituality movement have been deeply reinforced.

---

* Some numbers below do not add up to 92, and others exceed 92. This is because we could not readily label some people, and others mentioned several traditions and spiritual professions in their self descriptions.

We used a complex set of criteria to identify our "ideal" informants.

- *Variation.* We selected our key informants from as wide of a spread of the spirituality community as possible. Insofar as we could label them, we interviewed Catholics (n = 21), spiritually oriented Protestants of many stripes (n=28), Jews (n=5), Buddhists (n=5), Hindus (n=4), Native Americans (n=4), African Americans (n=3)[16], Muslim Sufis (n=3), and even a Basque teacher (n=1). We also sought out people who are making their own more idiosyncratic syntheses: we spoke with Zen Christians (n = 3), a transcendental meditator who leads psychotherapy groups, spiritually oriented psychotherapists (n=3), and so on. These and others had developed very complex syntheses: these folks we simply called "many" (n = 18).

In truth, the most common response to our question "what is your spiritual path" was laughter. Even if our people were predominantly Protestant or Jewish, they had all had wonderfully complicated paths. So our labels are at best approximations.

While no scholar is an expert in the full range of spirituality (this may be the first full-bodied study) it was clear to us that some scholars and sociologists of religion could offer great insights. Thus we spoke with or read many scholarly, especially sociological, informants (n = 25). We also selected out people who might be particularly knowledgeable about how spirituality is finding its way into our institutions: we talked with people who are actively bringing spirituality to business and government (n = 20), to medicine and the healing arts (13), and are working in the churches (n = 15). To make sure we were getting a picture of the whole "tribe," we also made it a point to interview informants from all five geographical sections of America: Northeast, Midwest, South, Southwest and West Coast.[17]

- *Role in the Spiritual Community.* We sought out people whose jobs or formal roles gave them access to some important facets of this community. We spoke with the leader of a Zen-Christian meditation group, for example, who saw people weekly, and thus might have an interesting view of why they were coming and what is going on in his or her corner of the spiritual community. We spoke with an editor of a journal devoted to spirituality and healing. We also spoke with or read the surveys and other researches of sociologists, who had a different kind of picture of this "tribe." [18]

- *Knowledge and communication skills.* In addition to having access to some facet of the spiritual community, we sought out informants who seem to have made *sense* of the information and were able to explain it intelligibly. It should come as no surprise that there are lots of sociologists, researchers or group leaders who may be wonderful at researching or leading meditation retreats, but who were not able to explain thing intelligibly.

- *Willingness.* Our conversations with people lasted at least an hour, and often two or three. We spoke with several people more than once. That's quite a commitment. Our subjects had to be both willing to spend this kind of time with us, and be available by phone. It says a lot about this community that only a few were unwilling to share their knowledge with us; indeed most offered to be interviewed again, should the need arise.

- *Openness.* Our ideal informants were able to share with us at two somewhat distinct levels. First, when we first asked them for their understanding of spirituality, naturally they shared with us the kind of formal talk they might share with any stranger or telephone interviewer: their public "rap." This of course has a value, for it is the kind of information someone might give in an introductory lecture, and as such was important for us to hear.

But our goals were more interesting. We were not after merely their superficial "rap" on spirituality, but something deeper. We wanted to know what spirituality is *really* about to these people, what they *honestly* think and feel after they have let their hair down. This intention was important to us: we wanted to know the real story, the motivating experiences, and the things that they were excited or concerned about. This is the kind of information that we thought could tell us what's really going on in our tribe. So after they had given their "canned" talk, we made it a point to probe them, ask them questions and seek clarifications. Once we had talked with them for awhile, we would ask them to clarify any inconsistencies, and to reflect in a variety of ways on their material. Thus we pushed and explored until we felt they had shared more of their "true" feelings, beliefs and motivations with us. Not all were able or willing to explore with us in that deeper, more open, level. But our truly "ideal" informants were.

To understand how we could get people to go to that more self disclosing level, it's important to tell you a little about us, the interviewers. Instead of hiring the typical recent college graduate to do our interviews, our interviewers were all mature and long term "members" of the Grassroots Spirituality Movement. Susan Jorgensen has been a Catholic spiritual director for many years, and was the editor of *Presence* the pastoral journal of Spiritual Directors International. A dedicated Catholic, Susan is a poet, is very well read in other traditions, participates in several small spiritual groups, and has worked in a range of churches and spiritual organizations. Kathryn Davison had recently received her Ph.D. in psychology, has explored a range of spiritual pathways since growing up a protestant in Texas, and was quite knowledgeable about spirituality, psychology and health. I, Robert Forman, grew up Jewish, have practiced Transcendental Meditation for more than 30

years, and have taught a range of religious/spiritual
programs at the university level for 18 years. Our subjects could really tell that we brought a range of mature
interests, backgrounds and long experience of spirituality to our conversations. Thus as we asked people to dig
under their "rap," we could do so because they saw us
as their peers. We tried to understand them well, and
they could tell that we were generally empathetic with
what they were saying. We believe people are more
likely tell their real story to peers. And so, we believe,
they did.

- *Selection procedure.* Anthropologists have developed a
  procedure to identify more strategic informants which
  they charmingly call the "snowball" procedure. This we
  also employed. We began with people of some renown
  in this movement. At the end of every interview we
  asked our respondents for names of others who might
  be particularly able to shed some light on this spirituality "tribe." In this way we built up a list of *recommended,*
  potentially strategic informants. We regarded each
  informant in our expanding list as having one or several
  useful perspectives on their culture, and if they satisfied
  our selection criteria, we tried to interview them.

- *Interview Procedure.* We used a standard, yet flexible
  interview procedure, the "structured free form interview." Interviews were structured in the sense that we
  began our interviews with a set of questions in mind.
  These we faxed or mailed to the informants ahead of
  time. Thus the interviewee knew roughly what subjects
  would be discussed, and it gave them a general frame-
  work to ponder. We also told them that not every informant would necessarily be asked to address every
  question. Everyone was asked to define spirituality, but
  from there we focused our conversations on the ques-
  tion(s) on which the informant might have particular
  expertise. With the structure clear, the informant was

allowed to explore our topics in any way he or she wished. If the informant veered too far from the subject however, the interviewer would interject comments, summaries or questions that were intended to bring them back to the topic, but without forcing them to adopt a predetermined pattern of conversation. This procedure encouraged our informants to explore their thoughts and insights in much more depth than the typical rote phone interview. We pursued relevant clues and suggestions, and we frequently asked them to clarify their thoughts, so that the informant was encouraged to explore the spirituality world in increasing depth. As the interview progressed, the interviewer would come to understand the interviewee increasingly deeply, and so we refined our ability to understand and explore their spiritual experiences, attitudes and lives with them.

The key informant technique, with structured free form interview, is designed to produce exactly what we sought; a general and qualitative portrait of the real beliefs, feelings and experiences of the Grassroots Spiritual tribe. It gave us an understanding of what is happening and why, and a clear sense of what our community understands as "spirituality." It is probably the best technique to show the general meaning, direction and "voice" of this enormous movement, and perhaps shed some light on its causes and functions.

However it does *not* show the *distribution* of any school, belief or attitude. Nor is it a good way to determine the size of individual sub-cultures of our tribe. For this we have to rely on surveys like Gallup's, Zinbauer's, Barna, Ray's and others.

Our goal was to learn who these spiritual people are, how they understand this world and spirituality when they are speaking openly, and then, from a position of understanding, to see if there are any patterns or commonalties to the range of techniques, insights, hopes and dreams that we heard.[19]

We expected a vast and fractured movement, with many contradictory beliefs. We certainly heard some contradictory opinions, especially in our interviewees' initial "raps." But when we scratched the surface of these thoughtful, experienced and sensitive souls, we found surprisingly profound agreement.

A Grassroots Movement?

We call this movement "grassroots spirituality." "Grassroots" does not imply that it's only taking place on the farms or on suburban grassy lawns. Nor do we mean to imply that it's happening only in the political grassroots, among political organizers, or within the ecology movement, though many within those groups are indeed exploring spirituality.

We call it "grassroots" to indicate that it has developed in a spontaneous and disorganized way among many everyday, ordinary people. Nobody has planned this growth. It is not coming from some religious authority or a Pope. No one is running this show.

This may be the first truly enormous religious-like system that has *not* had such singular leadership.[20] There has been no one Moses, Muhammad or Gautama Buddha. There are no official bishops, rabbinates or abbots. Thus we have to think about this large scale religio/spiritual movement very differently than the traditional systems with founders and/or organized structures. Grassroots movements, by their very nature, are messy. Their borders are highly permeable, and they contain complex and sometimes mutually inconsistent beliefs and attitudes.

But though this movement had no single founder, this does not mean it had no causes or that it is devoid of any leaders. Indeed there is an embarrassment of riches here. Many thousands have risen up, teaching to others what they have learned about this new way of thinking, meditating and living. They write books, lead weekend church retreats or conduct evening yoga kirtans. Some organize small groups, lead Bible studies or demonstrate Sufi dances. There are spiritual marriage counselors and folks who teach celibacy. Many transpersonal therapists, psychology of mind specialists and eating disorder counselors frame the human dilemma in spiritual terms. Others have religious titles: free thinking Jewish Rabbis, Catholic priests and chaplains, Protestant ministers and Sufi sheiks. This movement cuts right across the traditional/non-traditional divide.

In fact, a whole new "profession" has come up with strategies and titles as varied as this movement itself. We might call them "spiritual leaders and teachers." They are all helping people develop spiritual experiences and deepen life in their own special ways.

Many of these folks object to being called a "leader." They prefer "facilitators," "spiritual mentors," "spiritual friend," or the like. This is an expression of the egalitarian and anti- hierarchical mindset that runs through this movement. The logic here is that "unlike the priestly hierarchy, I don't claim to be spiritually higher or more privileged than those I teach." We're all on the path, all learning together.

By "leadership" then, let us be careful that we are not attributing a hierarchical attitude or claim of personal superiority to these folks. By "leadership" we merely mean those people who are actively helping others develop spiritually or are promoting the knowledge of spirituality in the world. "Spiritual" leaders are the folks who have written the books, sat in front of the meditation classes, led the prayer retreats, or the like. It is these people we interviewed and learned from.

Notes — Chapter II

[1] Quoted in IONS 1997 IONS Bulletin Conference Capsules, p. 13.

[2] George Barna, *Index of Leading Spiritual Indicators*, pp. 124–5.

[3] Zinnbauer, B.J., K. I. Pargament, and others. 1997. "Religion and Spirituality: Unfuzzying the Fuzzy". *Journal for the Scientific Study of Religion*, 36 (4) pp. 549–64.

[4] *Religion in America*, Gallup Report, May 1985, p. 50.

[5] Barna, p. 18.

[6] Robert Fuller, *Spiritual but not Religious: Understanding Unchurched America* (NY: Oxford, 2001), p. 4–5.

[7] Wade Clark Roof, *A Generation of Seekers: The Spiritual Journeys of the Baby Boom Generation* (SF: HarperSanFrancisco, 1993), p. 79.

[8] Paul Ray, *The Integral Culture Survey: A Study of Values, Subcultures and the Use of Alternative Health Care in America*, A Report to Fetzer Institute and the Institute of Noetic Sciences, Oct. 1995, pp. 77–8.

[9] Ray and Barna also mention another category, a middle group, whose constituents combine traditional religious views yet remain sympathetic to spiritual processes and religious mysteries. This comprises 26.8% of the population. Ray calls this the mainline Protestant (and presumably Jewish and Catholic?) pattern. Ray said these people's attitudes include the interest in the spiritual, but their beliefs and attitudes are highly various. We cannot say without further study just how many of this group might be part of this broad movement. So to be conservative, I will not count this number.

[10] Michael Hout and Claude Fischer, "Why More Americans Have No Religous Preference: Politics and Generations," American Sociological Review, Vol. 67, No. 2, April 2002, pp. 165–190.

[11] C. Kirk Hadaway, Penny Long Marler, and Mark Chaves, "What the polls don't show: a closer look at U.S. Church Attendance," *American Sociological Review*, 1993, vol. 58, (December) pp. 741–752. See also "Who really attends "church?" *The Christian Century*, vol 110 (Sept. 1993), pp. 848–9.

[12] Hadaway, et al, p. 748.

[13] Ibid, p. 749.

[14] Hadaway, et al, p. 748.

[15] Haut and Fisher, op cit.
[16] Three people mentioned that they were African Americans. We did ask about race in our interviews, thus there may have been more.
[17] While we did contact and read some non-Americans, our project was not designed to survey internationally; thus our sample was strictly American. See here the *State of the World Reports* (Washington, DC: Worldwatch Institute, 1994, 1995, 1996), and David Hay, op. cit.
[18] Here we should note that though we started by interviewing beginners and the spiritual "man on the street," we soon discovered that we were soon directed towards spiritual teachers and other leaders. But this means our data may be skewed towards the spiritual intelligentsia.
[19] We felt, and our subjects seemed to concur, that we really had understood them. But we want to acknowledge a possible methodological danger. It is possible that *we ourselves* formed the commonalties that we heard, that people were responding to our beliefs and assumptions. It is possible that they gave us, unconsciously or consciously, what we "wanted."

   This is possible, and indeed likely in such a survey to some extent. Our only rejoinder to this is that (a) we were surprised by what we heard, which suggests that we did not have these expectations when we began, (b) we only discovered the commonalties once we had finished the bulk of the interviews and were going through our database. (c) Four of us did the interviewing and each of us came to the project with different expectations. Yet the patterns we found were, on the whole, spread out among interviews conducted by all four.

   It is also possible that we simply picked and chose what we liked from within the database, and ignored what we didn't. Thus we may have supplied the commonalties in what we chose to include, after the interviews. This is always a danger in the construction of any scholarly model. Yet the surprising insights — about non-rationality, about the value of small groups, and about using small groups in the future — were to us unmistakable. We were struck *by* the commonalties, we felt, not the other way around. We hope that our ample use of quotes ameliorates this doubt.
[20] Here I think of the growth of early Hinduism as the nearest parallel. The Upanishadic thinkers, Gautama Buddha, the Ajivikas, and the Jains were all part of what seems to have

been a widespread cultural interest in new forms of thought. It is striking also that these systems that grew out of this interest were near to Grassroots Spirituality thought, for they too changed the Vedic ritualism towards systems that stressed personal and mystical experiences.

Chapter III

The Whispering Voices of Grassroots Spirituality

There is no better way to learn about this movement than to hear a few of the spiritual stories of several of our "key informants."

Sarah Rabinowitz:
Jewish Meditation Teacher

Sarah is a slim forty-something woman with a shock of curls and an easy smile. Her small apartment on the Upper East Side of New York City is decorated with Jewish memorabilia and an assortment of drums, glass bells and gongs that, she told me, her meditation groups use during their ritual prayer time. It's quite surprising, she tells me, chanting the Jewish "avodah" to gongs and drums.

My spiritual path started in the 60s, she began. I lived in the Siddha Yoga ashrams for a few years. But I found myself uncomfortable with the Sanskrit names and the Hindu forms of practice. I felt a conflict with my Jewish identity and the Jewish people.

Leaving the ashram was hard. Siddha Yoga is highly structured and I was used to that kind of regimented life. I had a lot of friends there. And finding something like a meditation group or an ashram within a Jewish context was hard. In fact, it didn't exist to my knowledge. I wasn't attracted to Havirah, the Jewish communal movement. Rather I wanted to enter into the depths of my Judaism. I had heard about Schlomo Carlbach who had founded a Jewish meditation group. It sounded like Carlbach had tapped a lot of teachings that were somewhat parallel to the mantra meditation and bhakti yoga devotional practices I had experienced in Siddha Yoga. So I thought I'd find out about it. I found the practices he used were effective, but I still wanted to bring out the teachings with a more Jewish theological orientation. So that's what I have been working to do. We have developed quite a few practices with that theological backing. The bells and drums help, but it's a Jewish practice. And I think they're pretty effective!

The reason I think we can use similar practices is that I think there is only one God, ultimately only one reality. Every tradition, every teaching has its own understanding and the practices they use flow from that. But the reality that all the traditions, practices and teachings point towards is the same one reality. Of that I'm sure.

I feel that Oneness as an expansive, wide open kind of experience. I feel sometimes a connection to God, to everything, for God includes everything. The key practice that we use to lead to that is what we call *bittel*. *Bittel* means nullification of the self, of the ego, and opening up to God, the reality, the truth. All our practices aim at that kind of nullification.

When people first open up their ego to the experience of the divine presence, they often feel unworthy, like they just don't deserve this. But the experience of the connection with God heals some of our early wounding. The hurts and anxieties and sense of unworthiness just fade away more and more. As they do, this process gives a sense of meaning and purpose to our lives.

People who have felt the first experiences of the divine presence of God in their lives often want to deepen this. So we give them Jewish practices that take them deeper. We have them meditate or pray longer, go deeper. They often tell me that they experience themselves as filled more and more with love. This we call the transformational Holiness deepening in them. This has happened to me. As I expand into the divine presence more and more, I find myself filled like that. My work gets deeper, my connections more intense.

In Jewish meditation practices we're expanding consciousness. There is an intention to do this before beginning prayer. There is a unification between God and the world, and it brings God's consciousness to the world. We fill the world with Godliness and His Oneness. Physics speaks of this unifying principle. God's reality *is* that unifying principle. This expresses itself as people becoming aware of their unity with each other and with that unifying principle.

Of course, there are other traditions. There is a schism between our various traditions, philosophies and practices. But I know, and I think we all know, that there are many ways to the ultimate, to God. We all have to be careful to not claim our way is the only way. We're all after the same experience of oneness. That's why people who are mystically oriented can feel close to people on other paths so easily, because our hearts are opening up in similar ways.

In fact, sometimes I feel closer to people on other paths than on my own. There's a mystical empathy or something that allows me to sense them, hear them, feel the commonalities.

That's OK with me. It's lovely in fact! The ultimate Jewish vision is a world which is filled with the awareness of God. It doesn't matter what word or phrase we use. It's the awareness of God, the knowledge of the unity with

"God's" expansive reality that we're all after. The paths are just different ways to discover this.

Doug Kruschke: "Pathways" Leader and Organizational Consultant

Doug Kruschke, fifty something, is a very successful organization development consultant in LA. He takes some pride in having worked with such corporations as Sony, the Disney family, a large automobile agency, Budget Rental, and so on. We sat on his large overstuffed couches in front of a corner fireplace.

Consultants generally can't talk directly of their spiritual path to their clients. For it a taboo subject in most corporations. So I think it was a particular pleasure for him to talk with me about it. He was hungry, he said, for company for this side of his life. Though he and his bright-eyed wife Diana lead "Pathways," an ongoing group to help people discern their own path, he himself had few peers with whom he could discuss his own spiritual quandaries or discoveries.

My path began in earnest in the United Church of Christ, he began. I thought I might be a nuclear physicist or a scientist. But after the sermon during one of those tent meetings, the minister called for people who wished to come forward to dedicate their life to Christ, become a minister. To this day I don't know what it was, but something just stood me up and called me to walk up to the stage. I had not even thought of this before, but there I was, walking to the stage. That was my first experience of the non-rational.

Afterwards I was embarrassed and didn't really know what on earth had happened. I denied the experience to everyone. But from it I got involved with a psychologically oriented Sunday school class. The guy that led it was dialogically oriented, which was quite unlike the lecture format that I had in my first experiences of religious communities. His class, and the retreat he took me on, got me interested in psychology and group dynamics.

Though when I entered college I fell away from the church, I had this inner sense of something guiding me. The church as an institution wasn't very important to me. But this sense of something bigger guiding me was. But as I studied psychology and got into graduate school in psychology, this sense kind of fell away.

In the 60s I tried psychedelics, which woke me up again to something bigger. I started reading Buddhism, taught myself meditation, and met Ram Dass. Buddhist philosophy seemed to catch it for me, a sense that I was on a path towards freedom. Something was going on in me. In retrospect I think I was trying to integrate these two sides of me, psychology and spirituality, which by now was largely Eastern.

With one of those breakthroughs you get in meditation, when you just open up, I remembered that experience I had had in that church, many years before, about dedicating my life to Christ. And I realized that I had been on a spiritual path all those years and that I was still searching for something I had not found through psychology.

So I began meditating for longer and longer times. As I did I found something was deepening. There was a sense of spaciousness and a gliding through life that I began to sense. There was an opening of some kind towards something beyond myself.

It was a feeling that who I am is all of it. That "it" that I was a part of became more real over time, that "it" was all there is. It was like "it" had, or I had, this semi-interested smile, that it cared about us, but not over-much. That "it" for me is what is true and real.

I still love to meditate. Melting out into that infinite space. I carry that spaciousness with me more and more.

My path is now one of integrating these two sides of myself, the psychologically trained side and the spiritual side. I love the Christian mystics, but I think of myself as a

Buddhist, if these labels mean anything. But really the challenge for me has been to weave my own psychological issues and personality together with this quiet, spacious, spiritual place.

I sense though that I could be more of what I am. There's a trajectory I sense in my life's development and I find myself still on it. It's like a continual settling and relaxing into who or what I am here and now. It's like coming back home.

The challenge for me is to help others find this coming back home in the way they interact with each other, in the way they relate with their spouses, in the way they relate with themselves. So my work in organizations and in communication is all centered on this possibility. That we can live the spirit in the way we interrelate with each other and with the world.

Somehow, and I'm not sure how, I know that my sense of my own life's trajectory is also a part of this universal that I can sense. I am becoming, and I think we are each becoming, more and more in tune with that as we clear our ego-stuff away. Our job is to break away the encrustedness and ride that inner core that's connected to that "It".

This is the grand project. It calls us all to grow up. That project is at the center of my life, of all of our lives I think. The grand project is not about getting wealthy, or being famous. It's about going beyond ego and getting in tune with the infinite beyond all our languages, our traditions and mostly all of our ego stuff.

I see my own life as moving more and more to allow the river of spirit to flow through me. Surrendering more and more to the flow and treating it as the most important element of life. To be spiritually mature is to realize that there is no one language or conceptual system that can contain this. It has to be lived, though it is beyond one system. Our systems, if we think they're it, can become a block to this. They can block the flow of spirit

The grand project then is for each of us to discover our place in the river of spirit. That place is becoming more and more important. It permeates more and more of my life and our culture. And it overflows into our spaces. It also says we can all live this way together. Now *there's* a grand project!

Robert Firestine: Martial Arts Master

A tall, handsome and well-built man in his late 30's, Robert exudes confidence. He is a martial arts teacher, the founder and director of the Universal Center in Tucson, which teaches Shoulin practices to children and young adults.

My path started when I was 16, he began. I took a walking trip across America with a "Walk across America for Disarmament and Social Justice" group. We were put up mostly in churches, Buddhist temples and other religious organizations. I remember even then being struck by the threads that I was hearing run through them. There is something that unites them all, I felt, something deep that is underneath the obvious separations and ethnocentrism. That perception of the deep threads began my life's direction.

At the core of the religions is something that unites. It is a unity, not a uniformity. It has to do with love and compassion, which relate somehow to that thread that underlies them all. The arguments and attempts at persuasion that religious people get into, these aren't the way to spirit. Love and compassion are so much better. I think that at their best the traditions and their rules are designed to lead believers to a sense of these core elements.

In martial arts, the masters don't argue. Their students do. The masters are just present and compassionate. They don't need to prove anything.

My path began in a Christian church but even as a kid I dropped out of that formal kind of path. Yet I needed some way to go, some sort of path. I was looking for something deeper. The practice of martial arts, I found, opened me up. I felt something great, larger than me, an enormous energy or something, would pour through me. It was very different from what I had known. We call that energy "chi", which means directing energy. Meditation, in combination with the martial arts, kind of clicked for me. With both I found myself opening up to that energy, opening up to spirit. There was an experiential communion with the spirit, with chi, through the vehicle of the body and the mind.

The phrase I like for all this is "become nothing and become something." We sit before martial arts practice as a way of touching this empty state of mind . . . and "become nothing." We take this empty state of mind onto the practice floor with us, and we carry it with us off the floor, into our day.

It's a sense of peace, a flow that allows us to act without effort. If you're there you don't get tired. You're one with the energy. It's a sense of peace, of joy. It carries a sweetness to life, a sense of harmony. At its clearest I lose a sense of boundaries. You can feel your connection to the trees or your surroundings. But you can also feel the vibration of this energy in your body, as if you can sense what's taking place in your own atoms. We're made of this energy; it is us, and the air and the earth. In fact, the air and the earth are in that vibration. They're both part of that energy and it is in them.

I've become closer and closer to these experiences over time. They happen more frequently. I am now working with my practices to make this sense permanent. Of course, we're in communion with God at all times. We don't lose it. But mentally, we lose it. So I am working at being present to it more and more of the time. It's more woven into the fabric of my life.

Of course I disconnect from it. When I'm angry, frustrated or in sorrow. But my work is to bring it even to those times, to allow love to be present even in my sadness. Some people want spiritual awakening to be only nice. But I think that my sorrow can allow me to open to others and to help them open. Many people want to be free of their pain. But I'm working on being open to the poignancy of pain. Even there I can sense spirit sometimes, and be into the flow of love and loss.

One day my wife went into convulsions. It was so hard to watch. But something opened up in me and I found myself just holding her and sending love. I knew she might die and that she was in pain. But strange as it may sound, I felt gratitude for being able to be there in love with her, open to the spirit that was running through us both. I felt only the joy of love for her. It was an honor to be there in such love.

Our spiritual awakening, opening to what is, can be there in moments like these, as well as on the practice floor. Our work is to be open to the spiritual presence all the time.

Evelyn Brush: Poet and Spiritual Writing Mentor

Evelyn began teaching high school English and writing in Chicago in 1970. Over the years she has become somewhat well known as a poet and a feminist, having begun the "Changing Writing Women" project which she describes as a celebratory feminist program. She quit her teaching job 4 years before we spoke with her. She now runs four classes of 15–20 adult women each term.

Raised Roman Catholic, she became frustrated with its patriarchal and anti-feminist character. She now calls herself a Unitarian Universalist. Her spirituality however centers not in a church but on her writing. Writing is a form of prayer, she said.

There is, she told us, within the brokenness of our lives a wholeness, a connection. It is a connection to what is. It's an integrity that you can't see but that you can sense. It lives beside loss and death, and integrates them with all of life. I can sense it not only in my head but in my whole self. It's a knowing of both head and heart. I used to think that I could know this only through my head, that is, with my understanding. But this evolved when I had to come to terms with a huge loss in my thirties. I thought I couldn't endure it. It was like a knife that carved out a space for me for compassion. I felt a spiritual power in that space immediately. I became certain that spirituality had to do with a level beyond the strictly academic or rational. In fact, when my teaching comes out of that place, there's a confidence I feel, a deep connection to what there is and to whom I'm teaching.

For me the spiritual life has to do with slowing down enough to pay real attention to that wholeness. It's out of that attention that I can really connect. The thing that helps me the most in this is my morning writing time. It doesn't matter if what comes out is great. But if I can just be centered, be present, then the rest of the day has a wholeness to it. It's as if I have found that connection between me and what is larger than me for a while. Then the rest of the day carries some of that. I write only for deep learning and connection. It's a practice for the rest of the day. It allows me to see that everything is infused with that connection, that meaning. I continue to write the text all the day long.

I also find that a spiritual community can help me to see what I believe and experience it mirrored in others. In our writing community, for example, this is strong. It's a sense of grace — that when I'm together with them something has been altered and multiplied in me and in the world. It's a kind of spiritual energy. I feel physically and emotionally different in community. When we sing, walk, meditate or are in silence, things are more aligned within me, like a compass.

This that I connect to is something like God, although I don't use that word often. I don't have a sense of Jesus or God. Rather I have a felt sense of this connection to something larger. It's more like a white light or a pure sound that I'm connected to. It's quite wonderful.

Kaz Tomo: Zen Roshi

For Kaz, who runs a Zen center in Texas, the term spirituality points towards "a way of life and mode of awareness that is in touch with the core of one's being." He was thinking here, he said, of the Zen term "kokoro", combined with "Shin." Koroko means heart or mind, that aspect of the self that is in the seat of both thinking and feeling. "Shin" he translates as spiritual. Thus the core of one's heart/mind, the core of one's being, means something that is both transcendent and immanent, beyond our egos yet inherent in what we are and what is in the world. To be in touch with this core of our being means we are in touch with the infinite field of reality what is beyond us, and from that vantage point to be able to critique our own ego concerns. It allows us to go beyond the self, yet also to embrace what is beyond us.

I try to live in a way that is centered in this, he told us. Doing so allows me to live in such a way that I can combine my Christian origins with my Zen training. In fact I find that the one energizes the other. It is the interiority of Zen that encourages me to experience going beyond my imaginings of the divine. It allows me to see beyond my own ego concerns and to experience and embrace that infinite field of reality. This enlivens my *kokoro*, it activates it if you will. To continue to practice of sitting Zen encourages me to be centered in the awareness of this core. Then to do the walking practice, *kinhin*, teaches us to continue that same attentive mode of awareness in our ongoing lives.

This way of being aware grounds me, grounds us, in the sense of unity with all there is. It encourages us to feel and to be compassionate with others. Thus compassion is a kind of test for what we experience. If we are more compassionate without self-consciously trying, it is a sign we're moving towards that sense of unity with all there is.

We all would like those more exotic aspects of the inner life as a kind of prize or goal. But this is just another kind of spiritual materialism, a craving for something. It's just another kind of ego-aggrandizement. If it stops there and doesn't lead to more ego-transcendence, more compassion, it becomes demonic. Whether the fruit of compassion is visible or not is the only way to discern if spirituality is really waking up and touching the core. Unless the inward experience plays out in activity, it's not yet realized.

We can think of vertical and horizontal dimensions of the spiritual life.

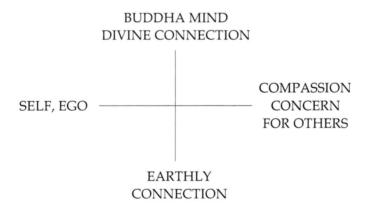

BUDDHA MIND
DIVINE CONNECTION

SELF, EGO

COMPASSION
CONCERN
FOR OTHERS

EARTHLY
CONNECTION

The Buddha Mind can be related to the Jewish and Christian term *ruach*, the breath of God, the Holy Spirit. These are the terms that stand behind the spiritual life. There are ancient traditions here. The central Divine reality, the breath of God, the *ruach*, can be related to the Upanishadic term *Atman* (whose root is also breath), and to the Chinese term *chi* (the term for energy which also points to the breath).

The point is that there is resonance here across the traditions. The term compassion points to the Christian idea that by their fruits you shall know them. Peace outflows from the contact with the divine as *agape*, the selfless love of others. The point is that spirituality naturally leads one to overcome the ego. God here is not something that one would identify with rules or ritualized names. Rather God is that which goes beyond all our egos. God is *sempre maior*, God beyond itself.

Of course, spirituality can become another ego trip. Many books and gurus are using it for self aggrandizement and to extend the ego. The signs of this are that someone presents themselves or their way of thinking as spiritual and the other not, a superior and divisive attitude, us versus them. In Zen we see people who reach a level of self-transcendence and recoil from that. They must let go, we tell them. It can be scary. But our work is to let go and find their freedom beyond the ego.

If what they experience, or if what someone teaches, leads them towards humility and compassion, then I take it as spiritual. If it leads to us/them thinking, for me it's a red flag.

Chapter IV

What is "Spirituality"?

---

*Take a pitcher full of water and set it down in the
    water
now it has water inside and water outside.
We mustn't give it a name,
lest silly people start talking again about the
    body and the soul.*

Kabir

*Then the Lord God formed a man of the dust of
the ground, and breathed (Lat.* spiritus*) into his
nostrils the breath of life.* [1]

When we began our research, our hypothesis was
that, as many people told us, we would find a
bewildering array of spiritual beliefs and patterns within
this movement. Several advisors warned us, "there would
be as many definitions or understandings of spirituality as
there are spiritual people." We fully expected that they
were right, and that we would find a very broad array of
definitions, tools and techniques, which would differ
depending on which tradition we heard from: the Jews
would stress God's commandments and practice
davening; the Christians would practice the Eucharist and
speak of Christ consciousness; the Buddhists would stress

empty mind and practice sitting, and so on. We saw some of this diversity among our examples in the previous chapter. But we hoped at least to be able to map these out, and find a range and pattern to the beliefs we saw, roughly like a spiritual geography.

But as we listened and went over our materials and listened some more, clear cut patterns and commonalities began to emerge. These consistencies became the basis of our definition of "spirituality." We noticed that there were some patterns in what was juxtaposed with "spirituality." . But then we began to see several common elements. In this chapter we will walk you through our layers of discoveries, spiraling down towards precision.

General Use of "Spirituality"

There were several patterns in the ways people used the term "spirituality." Our interviewees tended to use it in conjunction with terms like inner work, meditation, quiet, openness, aliveness. Doug Kruschke, for example, called the spiritual in himself that "quiet, spacious, spiritual place." Kaz Tomo talks of inner experiences which are validated in outward action. Thus in this usage, "spirituality" tends to have an introvertive, quietistic flavor. Generally it refers to the absence of thought or inner conflict. Robert Firestone spoke of "touching" this empty state of mind. But it can also be a very visceral sense, like being nourished or fed inside:

> "It's a kind of physical knowing, an internal body thing.
> It lives in my gut, radiating a sense of light and energy. I
> have a feeling of connectedness. It's energetic, empowering, and warm, like a dark, warm and energetic womb, a
> wide and nutritious space."[2]*

---

* Direct quotations from our interviewees will be put in italics. If we have received permission to use someone's name, we will footnote them by name. Otherwise we will use initials only. Quoted written material will not be in italics.

Thus "spirituality" carries the "inner" overtones we see in western and eastern meditative schools. Yet we were surprised how few people used the term "mysticism" in their definitions to us.[3]

A second common set of terms our interviewees associated with spirituality was whole, holistic:

"the broad meaning in life,"

"when 'It' lives me in everything I do."

"By becoming aware of our relationship to the whole and the way we've separated ourselves off from it, we see the whole."[4]

"There is amidst the brokeness of our lives, a wholeness, a connectedness, an integrity that you can't see but that exists."[5]

Thus spirituality points to more than just something introvertive. It also points to a change in our whole lives, or the sense of a deeper broad meaning to life.

The third set of associations we heard had something to do with connectedness and being in relationship.

"There is a relational character to spirituality. There are resonances, allurements, magnetic fields between things and people, connections between all things."[6]

"Spirituality is the inner awareness of self and its relation to the world around one. It is a consciousness of the self in terms of . . . its relational pattern to the world and others."[7]

Here spirituality implies something about being in relationship. It denotes a sense of connection with others, the world, and with the transcendent.

Finally people used the term in conjunction with a sense of being guided in some not-strictly-rational way. People tended to speak of the spiritual as the *not-strictly-rational*, the *non* linear, the "messy," or the un-knowing side of life.

"Spirituality has to do with a level beyond the strictly academic or rational."[8]

In a general way, then, spirituality seems to point to the intuitive, non-rational meditative side of ourselves, the side that strives for inner and outer connection and a sense of wholeness.

Spirituality versus . . .

In our second approximation of the term, we noticed that especially in their introductory "raps," our respondents often juxtaposed "spirituality" with some other term: the rational, the dogmatic, the institutionalized church, and the controlled.

Linguistically, then, "spirituality" tends to be a place-holder in a series of dualisms: The spiritual over against the rational, the dogmatic, the formal church, etc.

Most often, by far, spirituality was opposed to the "stuffy old church" and its fixed dogmas:

> *"People are very limited by their institutions, especially Christianity. People are feeling limited by it. . . . There is a sense of some freedom beyond that, which comes through moving beyond words. That is the spiritual."*

> One interviewee quoted Jung as saying, *"dogma, fixed verbalized beliefs, are obstacles to spiritual transformation."*[9]

> "Religion has come to mean believing the right dogma, praying in a perfunctory way, and avoiding actions, especially sexual. But spirituality is opposed to this. It points to a spiritual adventure."[10]

Thus "spirituality" is evoking that which is *other* than unmoving *dogma* or inflexible rules. We tend to speak of "dead, lifeless dogma," "the letter of the law," which we oppose to "living spiritual experience," the "spirit of the law" or the "living sense of the divine." One Christian teacher spoke of the *"dead or sinful flesh"* versus the lively spiritual center.[11] In a similar split, several Hindu-informed respondents opposed the living conscious *Atman* within the person to dead *prkriti* (nature).

People also tended to juxtapose the profane, especially the urban concrete and brick environment, with the more spiritual "natural world." Thus several described walking down a country path as spiritual, whereas no one found walking down a city sidewalk to be spiritual.

But our informants also tended to deny the very dualism they heard in their own words. After juxtaposing spirit with dogma or with the body, our respondents then declared that they did not wish to divide the world so sharply. Spirituality "also includes" the body, the church, and rationality, they said almost as an apology. In this we may be witnessing a theological shift reflected in our language use, for when people use a word differently, they're starting to think differently.

In the Beginning was the Word,
Spiritus

This use of the term "spiritual" as one side of a series of dualisms is in accord with the term's earliest etymology. "Spiritual" or "spirit" is cognate to the Latin *"spiritus,"* which originally signified air or wind. This term was used to translate the Hebrew *ruach*, (breath or wind) which signified the breath of God, and thus the vital, living breath within living beings. It was the *spiritus* (or *ruach*) of God that enlivened the "dead" clay of Adam: "Then the Lord God formed a man of the dust of the ground, and breathed (Lat. *spiritus*) into his nostrils the breath of life."[12] Thus from its earliest usage, *spiritus* was a placeholder in a dualism with "dead" matter.[13] We see this split throughout later Christian language, as in the famed "the spirit is willing but the flesh is weak." (Mt 26:41; Mk 14:38)

People of Hindu training tended to use the word "*Atman.*" In early Hindu thought *Atman,* the conscious human spirit, signified the similar side of a parallel split. *Atman* also meant wind or breath, and was occasionally opposed to *prkriti,* dead nature. Atman is also the consciousness within the human being that enlivens *jiva,* the mask-like personality.

Thus in all these uses, *spiritus* and *Atman* represent the living, conscious spirit as opposed to the non-living body or dead nature. Thus in our tendency to use "spiritual" as the more intuitive, living, or healthy side in a series of dualisms, we are inheriting its ancient etymology.

"Spirituality": A Definition

As we mentioned earlier, we did not expect to develop a single definition of "spirituality." But the agreement we heard was striking. It was as if many people were each giving us several pieces of a single, reasonably coherent jigsaw puzzle, and the pieces were fitting together nicely. Some gave us nearly all of the pieces, some just one or two. But it was one puzzle.

As Ludwig Wittgenstein taught, central complicated terms always are used in messy and confusing ways. As his example, he pointed to the many meanings of the term "game." Some games have clear rules, like baseball or soccer. Some have unclear and evolving rules, like kindergarten tag. Some have rules that seem to differ from one person to another, like the game of office politics. Some games are verbal, some physical. Some mathematical games are purely intellectual. Most high schoolers play the dating game, but poorly. Spouses often play a nasty game of one upmanship. . . And so on. Important terms are messy, and few ever have single phrase definitions.

So as you read the following definition keep in mind the following cautions:

1. As we listened we did indeed hear many different definitions. But few of them were as coherent or complete as ours. We are lending our own logic and coherence to the jigsaw puzzle that we heard.

2. There certainly *are* differences in the definitions we heard. Not everyone we interviewed will agree with every bit of our definition. We look at the definitions we heard as something like a Venn diagram or a jigsaw puzzle. Many of the definitions overlapped, many had only some elements in common, and some were very blurry. The Sufi will probably recognize some of the pieces we have identified, but not all, and the spiritual businessman may recognize other themes. Different folks can and will have varying attitudes towards certain pieces of the puzzle. Others, hopefully most, will resonate with all its pieces. But seen in this light, they are all part of the same overarching yet messy sense of "spirituality."

3. This definition is not prescriptive, but descriptive. It is not meant as some sort of new catechism, that if you believe this then you are spiritual, or some such rule. The Grassroots Spirituality Movement has no sharp edges. We offer it only because we heard this pattern among our 100 or so definitions.

Without further ado, our tentative definition is:

- *Grassroots Spirituality involves a vaguely panentheistic ultimate that*

- *is indwelling, sometimes bodily, as the deepest self and*

- *accessed through not-strictly-rational means of*

- *self transformation and group process*

- *that becomes the holistic organization for all of life.*

Grassroots spirituality involves a vaguely panentheistic ultimate . . .

This first phrase is the most problematic. Not everyone offered any particular doctrine of an ultimate at all. But when people did, calling it God, Allah, Brahman, the spirit, "It," or whatever, they lent it a vaguely panentheistic definition.

Panentheism is our only technical term. Please don't confuse it with *pantheism* (the doctrine that the deity *is* the universe and its phenomena). Instead, panentheism, (from pan + en + theos, lit., all in deity) is the doctrine that *all things are in the ultimate, that is, all things are made up of one single principle, but that one principle is not limited to those worldly phenomena.* For example, the ocean fish are made up entirely of ocean water and elements found in the ocean. The ocean in which they swim however is far bigger than only those fishes. Fish are *in* the ocean and it is *in* them, but it is not limited to the fish. The ocean then is "panentheistic" to the fishes.[14]

Thus the principle here is that all things and beings, including humans, are made up of a single "stuff" or substance. But that "stuff" is not limited to the beings in it. It includes but extends beyond them as well. It is both transcendent (in the sense of beyond) and immanent (within). As the early Hindu Upanishads put this, "having pervaded the universe with a fragment of myself, I remain."

> "*Spirituality is that ground out of which everything emerges. It is the One, the I am. We all have experiences of sprit; we recognize it, we are it. There is no separation between what we are and what it is. It is the whole that holds all the parts.*"[15]

The "whole that holds all the parts" implies that the whole is more than but includes those parts. This is perfect panentheism.

When Sarah Rabinowitz told us that she "feels some-times a connection to God, to everything, for God includes everything," she is using a panentheistic image. So too, when Robert Firestine said that he "felt something great, larger than me, an enormous energy or something, would pour through me," he is pointing to something that is both within him, pouring through him, and larger than him. This is panentheism. So is Kaz Tomo's notion of kokoro combined with shin:

> *"Thus the core of one's heart/mind, the core of one's being, means something that is both transcendent and immanent, beyond our egos yet inherent in what we are and what is in the world. To be in touch with this core of our being means we are in touch with the infinite field of reality, what is beyond us,"*

Similarly, if the "spiritual includes all" it is panentheistic:

> *"The spiritual includes everything. It is a divine energy that flows in us and through us."*[16]

> *"A spiritual person is conscious of his connection with the wider lifestream."*[17]

It may be natural for people trained in Eastern reli-gions — Advaita Hinduism, Buddhism, Taoism, etc. — to hold such a doctrine, for panentheism is traditionally taught in these schools.

But we were surprised when we heard Christians, Jews and Muslims describing their sense of the ultimate in panentheistic terms. In fact, it was this that convinced us that panentheists may now be the general view, or major-ity report. For this is by no means traditional. In fact, it used to be heretical! The panentheistic writings of Medi-eval Christian mystic Meister Eckhart were declared to be heretical by the Pope in 1328. Others were burned at the stake for making similar claims. Al Hallaj was decapitated and quartered by the Muslim authorities for making panentheistic assertions. The shift here is striking![18]

For example when one devout Catholic, said, "*we are in that energy source from which all emanates,*" she was stating a panentheistic doctrine.[19] Another Catholic told us, "*As a child, I thought of God as 'out there.' But I don't now. [Now I think that] everyone has the presence of God within them. . . . Now I think that God permeates everything.*"[20] Another Catholic described this panentheistic ultimate as like an ocean in which she swam or like a nourishing amniotic fluid, a wonderful image for panentheism:

> "*God's presence is everywhere . . . all over. It is my capacity to perceive it that is limited. . . . The closest image for God is my experience of being in the ocean with no swimming suit on. . . . It is like a universal energy field, the divine amniotic fluid, life force. It is the One in whom we move and live and have our being.*"[21]

A Christian minister spoke similarly:

> "*Spirit is not only indwelling but everything else is in it as well. It's all around you as well as indwelling. While my experience of it is within me, I sense this as everything IS God in a real sense. There is no ground without a substratum of God. . . My life's work, my motive, is to move more and more towards or into this spirit or God. The goal of life is for each of us to have a primary experience of God.*"[22]

Other Christians described a similar doctrine, calling it "Christ consciousness."

Similarly, Jews of various stripes described a divine principle—which they called *ruach*, breath or wind. Kaz Tomo said that in this *ruach* we all reside, and it breathes within us. Another told us,

> "*we feel that the divine in the universe is calling on us to move away from old ways of connecting with God as king and judge, towards metaphors that are much more intimate — the <u>ruach</u>, the breath of life for example.*"

Another Jewish respondent spoke of a panentheistic spiritual ultimate as

> *a formless, eternal reality that lies at the heart of all forms. It's something that is one, beyond our usual apprehension of space and time. . . It's experienced within us as well, often during prayer time. It's like quietness within, the still point of the turning world.*[23]

A Muslim Sufi leader described a clearly panentheistic ultimate:

> *Spirit is behind everything. It is the hidden aspect of nature. Everything is a crystallization of spirit. It is seen behind everything. Spirituality is looking beyond the surface, being in touch with the living energy. The spirit is the source behind everything we see, the invisible energy behind it all. There is one living source, which manifests in innumerable ways. It takes a unique shape in each person.*[24]

Jews also call the panentheistic infinite *M'kor Hayyim*, the Wellspring of Life.

We were also surprised to hear Buddhists espousing a panentheistic doctrine. Though an Eastern school, Buddhists traditionally teach a doctrine of *shunyata*, emptiness, which is not traditionally presented as "stuff-like" at all. But several of our Buddhist informants clearly spoke of a panentheistic ultimate. One creatively presented it in terms of the famous Zen phrase "mind and body disappearing":

> *"Buddhism talks of mind and body disappearing. This sounds like a negative expression. But its not nihilism. It is through this negation that life emerges. When as the Buddhists say, you disappear, then "It" lives me. To experience life and to get to the positive, you must let go of self, mind and body. When mind and body disappear, it's like being part of God. Think of how it was for Adam and Eve. They were part of God. They were happy to be*

part of God. But when they began observing the self, they
separated from God. We practice letting go through med-
itation, and now we live this life as part of the whole."[25]

This notion of "living life as part of the whole" and "being
part of God" are clearly panentheistic thoughts.

There were important exceptions to this panentheistic
"majority report." As noted, some did not want to speak of
an ultimate at all. Our Native American or Basque spirituality contacts did not present a panentheistic doctrine.
These people did not tend to describe a single principle,
but rather something more like a series of links or a web
that interconnect us all. Their preferred image looks more
like a web than an ocean. One wise primal thinker said
"*there is a relational character to spirituality.*" When we
asked her, is this panentheism? she replied that no, this is
not quite the same as panentheism:

> "*There is an energy around each and every thing. The*
> *rock or this table has spirit. It's more like a set of intercon-*
> *nections. There are resonances, allurements, magnetic*
> *fields between things and people. There is a connection*
> *between all things. . . . Spirituality is an integrated,*
> *interconnected combination of people and things that*
> *join in relationship to each other to explore the gift of*
> *life.*"[26]

To such people as her, we are all enmeshed in a series of
connections, and our lives can be guided by the "spirits"
that we find around us. Our shaman contacts teach the
same thing.

Such a doctrine is not quite panentheistic, but it is strikingly close, is it not? We still have interconnectedness.
There is a sense of being enmeshed in something broader
than we ourselves. The sacred is still non-verbal. The difference here is over the question whether the sacred is
something like a single extended thinking, or more like a
series of links or a web between discrete things.

In nearly all our informants, then, the parallels are far more surprising than are the differences. *Strikingly, not one single person* offered the traditional western view of a transcendent father or mother figure. *No one* suggested that God is distant or separated from humanity, like a judge. No one described a being that offered heavenly rewards. No one used the transcendent God language, like that still dominant in most churches, synagogues and mosques, or in the more fundamentalist side of the great cultural divide. We heard no God- as-Father language. No one suggested that after we die God determines our procession to Heaven or Hell. Considering that this was the dominant model less than a century ago, it is astounding that we never heard it. Not once. In fact, this may be one of the critical hallmarks separating Grassroots Spirituality from more traditional religious systems.

The exception proves the rule. The few who spoke of God as a "Holy Other" made it a point to define it panentheistically. Note how thoughtful Christian minister M.I. moved from describing an indwelling "other" to a panentheistic something that connects him to everything:

> "This knowing experience of spirit is a sensing of the 'other.' Spirit or God is 'other' in the sense of its being sentient. 'It' knows me. In it I have the sense that I am loved. It's a primary relationship that comes without words. Though my experience of it is in me, still I know I didn't generate it from inside me. It is part of me, within me, yet my experience of it is as something that is 'not me.' It leaves me with the feeling that I am connected to everything and everyone. Its unity is my connectedness."

Here M.I. subtly combines the sense of its otherness with a notion of an indwelling something through or within which he feels connected to everything. In effect, he is interweaving a traditional Christian view with a more panentheistic (and Grassroots Spirituality) sensibility.[27]

Michael Lerner, editor of the journal, *Tikkun,* also creatively combines traditional transcendental deity language with panentheism when he wrote,

> "There is a power, a presence, a force in the universe — indefinable, unknowable — that pulls us towards transcendence. That tremendous creative and healing power, or presence, is what many of us call God, or Ultimate Reality. Its nature is kindness, compassion and love — in all its forms and manifestations. . . . that transcendent reality . . . is both within us, at the core of our being, and all around us, saturating every part of this sacred universe."[28]

When Lerner speaks of a force, a healing power, whose nature is love, he speaks with traditional theistic language. But he rapidly modulates this into a more panentheistic tone with "that transcendent reality . . . is both within us, at the core of our being, and all around us." Like M.I., Lerner is creatively refilling old wine skins with a new wine.

Of course, panentheistic language is not entirely new. It can be found in many traditional writings. What is new today is a consistent presentation of such a panentheism in our Grassroots Spirituality community.

In short, the traditional western "transcendent" model of God is no longer operative in the Grassroots Spirituality Movement. Its Ultimate is reminiscent of the omnipresent, immanent yet infinitely extended vacuum state of quantum physics, more like an "It" than a "He" or "She." In "It" "we live and move and have our being."[29]

This shift from a personal view of God as transcendent to an ultimate panentheism is profound. It is one of the keys that separates this movement from the mainline belief systems that have been with us for so long, and one of the things that distinguishes it from Conservative Christianity. Its implications are certainly as deep as the shifts from the commanding Hebrew Lord to Christianity's triune God of faith, the shift from ancient China's heavenly "Shang-Ti" to Taoism's indescribable Tao, or the shift from Vedic pantheism to the Upanishad's monistic Brahman. The Grassroots Spirituality movement now understands each of us as more interconnected to the whole and to the Divine principle than did our ancestors who believed in a transcendent deity.

Because we no longer think with a hierarchical king model, this theology now fits, like a key in a lock, with our democratic and egalitarian mindset. For in this panentheistic view no one thing is supreme. All are, if subtly, part of the same One, and thus all equals. We now regard ourselves as part of an endless interconnective spiritual tissue.

There is an insight in this new doctrine. If we could all find ways to express this ultimate by working — playing — together it would say something important in the world. If we can realize our inherent interconnections, or better still, express these connections in our actions — and these are big ifs — we may come to experience ourselves in very spacious, pacific ways. If Jew, gentile, Muslim, agnostic, Buddhist and Christian all could see ourselves as part of the same underlying fabric, it would be hard to go to war with each other. This doctrine offers a profoundly optimistic view of human life — and may portend a more hopeful future — if we can together capitalize on this new theological attitude. But of course, this is a very big if.

One last point: our informants often left this panentheism as if intentionally *vague*. Few of our informants explored the nature of the ultimate in the kind of verbal detail we have just provided. Grassroots Spirituality, as we will see, in part emerges from a frustration with rationality and dogma. Few therefore felt the need to give carefully "rationalized" accounts of the ultimate. People almost intentionally leave it unexplained and fuzzy. We heard "The Tao that can be spoken is not the eternal Tao" several times. *"My spirituality is rooted in ambiguity."*[30]

Indeed, one of our informants suggested, it may be that this vagueness is a systematic way to allow people to hold mutually incompatible beliefs or to participate in several different traditions at once without being bothered by verbal differences. If I want to hold to both a personal deity and also to an impersonal spiritual principle, what better tool than vagueness?

That is indwelling, sometimes bodily, as the deepest self . . .

If there is a single panentheistic ultimate in which everything rests and which indwells within everything, then it must also indwell within us. And indeed our subjects do generally teach that it does. People hold that there is some deep but hidden level *within us* that connects us to the infinite ultimate. As Ewert Cousins, editor of the *Encyclopedia of World Spirituality,* puts this,

> "The spiritual core is the deepest center of the person. It is here that the person is open to the transcendent dimension; it is here that the person experiences ultimate reality."[31]

Here, the spiritual core resides deep within us, at our core. Yet this core connects us to what is beyond as well. We heard this indwelling ultimate called many things: Meister Eckhart's "divine spark" was quoted by several. Christians called it the "indwelling God" or "the Christ within." Hindu trained meditators called the indwelling principle their *Atman,* or *Purusha,* the infinite and deeply satisfying conscious silence (*satcitananda)* at their depths. Our Jewish informants spoke of the *"shechinah,"* the indwelling divine or the feminine principle of God, which, one said, *"indwells within us all as the very breath of life."*[32] And Atman, in turn, connects to *Brahman,* the world essence.

This is often described or felt in very bodily terms. Notice the bodily sense of the following, already quoted:

> *"It's a kind of physical knowing, an internal body thing. It lives in my gut, radiating a sense of light and energy. I have a feeling of connectedness. It's energetic, empowering, and warm, like a dark, nurturing and energetic womb, a wide and nutritious space."* [33]

One woman described an experience in her spiritual group:

> *"Everything people said was going through my body ... I thought "holy smokes!". ... That's a good way of putting it ... it's a powerful but vague feeling."* [34]

This deepest aspect of the self may be described as like a well which reaches down to a vast water table below. We gain access to the wide spiritual waters by diving down through this well at our inmost core. *"Having contact with God within brings one to a reality that is beyond oneself and yet, at the same time, speaks from within."* [35] And, people often point out, if we perceive such an endlessness, we may come to recognize that everything about us and about the world is composed of it.

Michael Lerner, editor of *Tikkun*, wrote,

> "At heart, our deepest desire is to realize our oneness with that power, that transcendent reality that is both within us, at the core of our being, and all around us, saturating every part of this sacred universe." [36]

But, we heard over and over, we do not generally sense this deepest inmost level. Why not? It is our own preconceptions, rational minds, and primarily our *attachments* (ego, greed) that keep us from generally realizing this deepest principle.

> *"We all have the capability of sensing spirit, an intimate part of us. But certain kinds of behavior inhibit or block*

it. Judging, casting our boundaries tightly around me
and mine, etc."[37]

"It is our ego that stops us from knowing 'this.' The
indwelling divine is not my ego, it's not my (rational)
mind. Spirituality is not a product of my ego. It's appears
in that part of me that is made in that image of God space,
where there is a trembling of the holy."[38]

"The spirit of God is the very stuff of our soul, really what
we are, after we peel the veneers off."[39]

D. H. Lawrence beautifully captures this sense of getting
out of our ego:

When we get out of the glass bottles of our ego,
and when we escape like squirrels turning in the
    cages of our personality
and get into the forests again,
we shall shiver with cold and fright
but things will happen to us
    so that we don't know ourselves.
Cool, unlying life will rush in,
and passion will make our bodies taut with power,
we shall stamp our feet with new power
and old things will fall down,
    we shall laugh, and institutions will curl up like
burnt paper. [40]

This sense of an "indwelling" One has an implication for
our religious structures. If we each are gifted with an
indwelling spark of the One, then we have no need for
some mediating figure like a priest or a minister. For "It" is
already available to each of us. Nor do we need an interces-
sor, for it's available to us by merely letting go of our attachments. If we're each connected to the All through some
deep inner wellspring, then no one of us is more connected
to "It" than is any other.

This in turn points to the new kind of leadership we
have already noted: the priesthood of the many. Each of us

is implicitly connected to the Whole and to our own wisdom. Each of us can be, in a sense, our own mediator with the Divine, our own priest. If we can only tap into our inner core wellspring, we can each gain access to the sacred infinite. All we need is deep and steady enough self-discovery to extract ourselves from the glass bottles of our egos.

Thus the growth of self-reflection, meditation and of small spiritual support groups, are, as we will see, some of the most popular tools of this movement. These are natural expressions of this "theology" of the indwelling. For through these we can, in theory, discover and guide our own and others' spiritual growth. Thus it is natural that this movement is non-hierarchical. It makes deep sense that so many Grassroots Spirituality leaders would deny making hierarchical claims for themselves.

But again the movement needs and has leaders. Its leaders do not present themselves as priests performing sacraments on our behalf or making intercessions. More commonly, they present themselves as merely more experienced on the path. It is striking that, though many are involved, at the forefront of this movement are neither ordained priests nor gurus.* It seems to us that the best leaders of this movement must hold their leadership roles lightly and humbly. Any guru for Grassroots Spirituality must always remain an unguru.

And is accessed through . . . self transformation and group process

In short, members of this movement hold that there is some spark of the infinite indwelling within. But it remains veiled from our eyes. We don't generally recognize or realize its presence. Therefore we must undergo

---

* Matthew Fox is the one exception to this rule. But tellingly, he was asked to drop his role as an official priest.

some kind of transformation process so that we can discover it and bring it into our lives more effectively.

As we began our researches, we had expected that people would talk of this process as one of *self*-transformation.
And so they did, often. One can and must work on this
growth through meditation, we heard, inner work, therapy, body work and other individual processes. We must
actively free ourselves from our attachments, we heard,
our egos, or from the hold of our beliefs and stuck places.

Ongoing and open ended growth was a leitmotif of our
interviews. Some spoke of their history of self analyses,
psychotherapy, marriage counseling, and the self-track-
ing processes of certain meditation techniques, reading or
the like.

Thus spiritual development is often said to be like a
journey. Frances Vaughan captured it best when she said
that we must undergo a "process of unfolding, of awakening, of reclaiming the true self. . . . Thus spirituality is like a
path or a way."[41]

But in addition to such solo inner work, we were surprised how many people of our interviewees stressed
group work. It is an important piece of the modern spiritual
journey. The recent Jewish Renewal movement, for example, emphasizes *havurah*, the fellowship found in small
communities.[42] Catholics are organizing with what
Arthur Baranowski calls "Small Christian Communities:"
intimate church-organized small groups and "house
churches" through which people explore their lives and
beliefs in intimate settings. Many successful Protestant
churches have discovered that small Bible Study groups,
adult Sunday School classes, support and self help
groups, and other small intentional groups enliven spiritual lives and through them, the churches themselves.[43]
While it is centered on a single issue, priestly pedophilia
and the bishop's cover-ups, the recent grassroots Catholic
movement, Voice of the Faithful, is tapping this instinct.

Many of our informants stressed that their small group and/or their informal set of colleagues and friends have become very important aspects of their spiritual lives.

"Spirituality requires finding some time for me. But it also means finding people in my life who will show up for me and give me an ear."[44]

"Keating's centering prayer that seeks to be in the presence helps my spiritual life a lot. But I also have a great need for being in relationship. The soul matures through ... dialogues and connections."[45]

Others simply stated that they longed for such community or connection. Some even defined spirituality in terms of relationship:

"Empathy is a core component of spirituality. We have a yearning for oneness, whether it is with another human or with the divine within, or a yearning for oneness with nature."[46]

De Tocqueville noticed long ago that even though American society is profoundly democratic and ruggedly individualistic, it is also one in which we band together to solve our problems. This paradox is now shaping our spirituality as well. We are both sounding our own inner depths, and also intimately supporting and guiding each other, relying on both our own and on each other's wisdom.

This focus on intimate groups is both an answer to our spiritual hunger and a response to the loneliness of a mobile and impersonal society. When we no longer share backyards with a steady coterie of neighbors or relatives, the small group is one possible answer. It can be intimate yet not life long; it can survive some members moving away, and it provides a forum to explore intimate issues.

Considering the enormous role that distant, sometimes intimidating priests, rabbis, ministers, gurus, and community shamans have played through the centuries, this small group model is another astounding shift. In our new willingness to each discover our own path, articulate our own insights, and in our ability to help each other, we have learned to sound the spiritual depths without relying on some mediating hierarchical authorities. Perhaps this was inevitable, considering how educated, self confident, autonomous, and open to transformation is this community. Thus Grassroots Spirituality is a new and natural outgrowth of this particular population.

And accessed through . . . not strictly rational means

However they have learned to overcome their ego and loosen the hold of their dogma, our informants emphasized that the spiritual transformation process is **not strictly rational**. "The *nature of spiritual understanding, that life-enlivening principle, is beyond the strictly logical."* [47] Often it is said to involve going beyond rationality and dogma. *"Dogma, fixed verbalized beliefs, is an obstacle to growth,"* Jung was quoted as saying. *"You must go beyond linear thinking."*

> *"Spirituality is a living dynamic or meaning, not an answer. It lives side by side with loss and death, not an answer only of the head alone, but a knowing of the head and the heart. It has to do with a level beyond the strictly academic. When my [work] comes out of that place, I notice a confidence but not arrogance, a deep connecting."* [48]

After his experience of walking up to the stage to state his interest in becoming a minister, Doug Kruschke said,

> *to this day I don't know what it was, but something just stood me up and called me to walk up to the stage...That was my first experience of the non rational.*

We have chosen to call this aspect of spirituality the "not-strictly-rational." Transpersonal psychologists Ken Wilber and Frances Vaughan prefer the term "trans-rational." By this they mean a process that is "beyond but inclusive of" rationality. When we ran this term by our some of our informants, however, most did not know or understand the term. Those that did pointed out that it seems to suggest some kind of mental hierarchy: something like animal emotions, regular thought, higher thought, and highest of all, trans-rational experience. If so, they said, they were not comfortable with its implicit hierarchy.[49] Can human life and thought be separated and hierarchically ranked like this, they wondered? Some even wondered if there is any intelligibility at all to the process: *"Does the work of "God," one asked, "include our rationality? It may be entirely unrelated to the way we rationally think. Just what leads to an epiphany is not at all clear."*[50]

All could agree, however, that, whatever the process, it is certainly not strictly rational.

Whatever we call it, it is striking how novel is this whole attitude? Christians fought for centuries about the correct way to understand the Divine, even going to war over the way to rationally conceive of God and the words of the liturgy.[51] Theravada Buddhists struggled for centuries to specify just which of a few dozen "dharmas" stand behind experience. Confucianists bickered over the precise nature of the true *zhunzi*, gentleman.

But here we are, at the pinnacle of perhaps the most rational and technologically developed civilization in history, and our Grassroots Spirituality movement resists the whole rationalistic bugbear altogether. "Live from the right side of the brain" . . . "transcend thought" . . . "synchronicity" . . . "turn off your computer, Luke, and trust the Force" — these are our new watchwords. In our spirituality we are repudiating our "logical" macroeconomic schemes and our computerized workstations, and we strive to open ourselves up to the not- strictly-rational.

The long term effects of such a sea-change in the history of thought are hardly imaginable. Clearly it will have an effect on how we conceive of learning, working, governing and playing. It already shapes countless movies and books.[52]

That becomes the holistic organization for all of life

"Spirituality is the shape of one's life as a whole," writes etymologist Richard Woods, OP, "particularly as integrated around a core set of beliefs, values and practices that are to some degree generally religious."[53]

We heard this notion of holism, whole and holistic a lot. One of our interviewers, Susan Jorgenson, a Catholic spiritual director, defines spirituality simply and elegantly as *"wholeness making."*[54] It is generally held that in order for spirituality to be complete, it must eventually guide the whole of our lives.

> *"Many of us are called to living a spiritual life that is not separate from the world. [It is to] live life as a daily practice in relation to the creator."*[55]

> *"Spirituality involves living one's life in relationship with God. Every decision we make should reflect our relationship. In fact, it should be reflected in our whole life style."*

In this way spirituality becomes a guiding value orientation for our whole lives. We want to have everything become oriented around this. *"The challenge is to make spirituality relevant to everything we are, where and who we are right now, in everything we do."*[56] A Christian finds this sense in the command to *"love God with all your heart."*[57] Spirituality for us today must be discovered in the everyday. As Zen Roshi Charlotte Joko Beck puts this, it must be "everyday Zen."

"When I am living a deeply spiritual life, I am aware that something more is happening. We are more than what we are feeling at that moment. . . . The more is a peacefulness that allows me to be less rattled in everything I do. It's like holding onto an unflappable center. . . like a fireman's pole."[58]

We want to orient the whole of our lives, including all its complex roots, around these principles:

Roots and wings —
but let the wings take root
and the roots fly.
                    — Juan Ramon Jiminez

This can be understood as a kind of guidance for life. A Shaman informant points out that this *guidance for life can be very specific and directed by spirit beings.*[59] Others point to a vaguer sort of guidance, like the psalmist's suggestion that God will somehow "guide your feet on his true path."[60]

Many told us that they wanted these deep values and their sense of life's meaning to be experienced in their everyday family lives, in their workplaces, and in all of their days.

"'Spirituality' is a stupid term. Everyone is talking about it, but who knows what it means? . . . Holistic is better. But I am much more interested in the story of everyday life, which is all about the ordinary events of a life. . . The greatest awakening for me as a spiritual being came when I was folding diapers. Before then my idea of spirituality was about getting away, going to a monastery, going to church. But then I realized that the act of folding diapers is a spiritual act."[61]

Pirsig's famous *Zen and the Art of Motorcycle Maintenance* makes the same point.

In general then, the Grassroots Spirituality movement holds that there is wisdom inherent in the spirit. Its mem-

bers seek to allow that wisdom to guide them in everything. *"I want to bring my greater self, not just some narrow
band, into everything I do. My [professional] work is just
another arena for my spiritual growth. [For those of us] in the
business world, this is just part of the growth of our evolution."*[62] They hold that there is something wise about this
spiritual side of life. It has a built-in wisdom. It, the
panentheistic indwelling ultimate, seems to have an inherent wisdom woven into its very nature that can provide an
orientation for everything they do. If, that is, one can
realize it.

Conclusions

Many within the Grassroots Spirituality Movement will
disagree with elements of our definition. We look forward
to such a discussion, for it will be inevitable and healthy.
But despite the predictable wrangles, the point is this:
though we hail from virtually every major religious and
spiritual tradition from around the globe, though we have
very different vocabularies, traditions and perspectives,
members of this Grassroots Spirituality movement share a
worldview in far more depth and even specificity than
most have recognized.

The impression that there are deep and irreconcilable
differences between adherents of different spiritual pathways is probably due more to the centuries of religious
bickering than to the beliefs of today. It was the long history of institutional squabbles, I think, that led us when
we began to expect irreconcilable differences. Rabbis or
priests have vested interests in articulating and defending
what differentiates them and makes them special. They
may be driven to differentiate theological lines for personal, professional and institutional reasons. Many spiritual people, who have little or no investment in those
institutions, seem to have come to a largely unrecognized
common set of attitudes: the sense that a panentheistic

ultimate surrounds and infuses all our traditions and all our lives, and that we can first discover it within.

"The history of religions is that religions tend to divide people one from another. The history of spirituality is that spirituality cuts across barriers."[63]

Whatever the reason, despite our expectations when we began this study that we are all singing different songs and holding to different worldviews, those in the Grassroots Spirituality Movement now share a worldview and even techniques to a far greater extent than we knew.

One important implication of this definitional exercise is this: people from many different traditions share *enough* of a worldview that they should be able to *communicate in some satisfying depth with one another.* In talking about modern day Sufis, renewal Jews, and spiritual business people, we're not talking about apples, spare tires and machine guns, but something more like Red Delicious, Macintosh and Granny Smiths.

Many people told us, as we noted, that they longed for long term and deep dialogues between committed spiritual people from a variety of paths. Given the surprisingly deep level of agreement we discovered, no matter which tradition they hail from, folks in this movement should be able to communicate relatively easily with each other. Their challenge — and privilege — lies ahead.

Notes — Chapter IV

[1] Genesis 2:7
[2] Susan Izard
[3] Perhaps, as one put it, they felt that would connote a weird-ness they wanted to avoid.
[4] Glenna Gerard
[5] MPB
[6] Angeles Arrien
[7] Wade Clark Roof
[8] Evelyn Brush
[9] JH. We were not able to verify this quote.
[10] David Ray Griffin, *Parapsychology, Philosophy and Spirituality* (Albany: SUNY Press, 1997).
[11] CP
[12] Genesis 2:7
[13] For the substance of this paragraph, we are indebted to Richard Woods, "Spirit and Word," *Presence* Magazine, 1996.
[14] Another term for panentheism is the even more confusing "trans-immanent."
[15] Glenna Gerard
[16] BLS
[17] RW
[18] The accusations against such people grew out of a need, I believe, to protect the absolute difference and thus author-ity of Jesus, the church or mosque, etc. If Eckhart or Al Hallaj experienced what Jesus or Muhammad did, why should one obey the eccliastical authorities?
[19] Susan Jorgensen
[20] Nick Wagner
[21] JM
[22] MI
[23] Tony Stern
[24] Suhrawardi Gebel
[25] Janet Abels
[26] Angeles Arrien
[27] MI
[28] Michael Lerner, related to us by Rachel Harris.
[29] Acts 17:28. See Capra, *The Tao of Physics* for a similar obser-vation.
[30] MPB
[31] Ewert Cousins, Preface, in *Christian Spirituality, vol. 1,* ed. Bernard McGinn, John Meyendorff and Jean Leclercq (NY:

Crossroads, 1987), p. xiii. See here also W. H. Clark, *The Psychology of Religion* (New York: Macmillan, 1958): Spirirituality "can be most characteristically described as the inner experience of the individual when he senses a Beyond, especially as evidenced by the effect of this experience on his behavior when he actively attempts to harmonize his life with the Beyond" (p. 22).

[32] AW
[33] Susan Iznard
[34] Wuthnow, p. 264.
[35] MWC
[36] Micheal Lerner, quoted to us by Rachel Harris.
[37] MI
[38] Felicia McKnight
[39] Bill Farley
[40] Angelo Ravagli and CM weekly, the complete poems of D.H. Lawrence, (NY: Viking Penguin Books, 1964.)
[41] Frances Vaughan, *Shadows of the Sacred* (Wheaton, Ill: Quest Books, 1995), p. 7.
[42] Riv-Ellen Prell, *Prayer and Community: The Havurah in American Judaism* (Detroit: Wayne State University Press, 1989).
[43] The best resource on these small, religiously organized small groups is Robert Wuthnow.
[44] BR
[45] Charles Simpkinson
[46] RE.
[47] CP
[48] MPB
[49] Here especially see the work of Jorge Ferrer, who takes issue with Wilber's implied claim that religious development has a consistent developmental model.
[50] SJ
[51] Not to be oversimple, but the wars of the Reformation were in deep ways centered on this question. The conflicts between Eastern and Western christendom were also centered on rationalistic ways of articulating the divine.
[52] See Tony Stern's, *Mystical Insights of the Silver Screen*, forthcoming.
[53] Richard Woods, SJ, "Spirit and Word," *Presence*, 1996.
[54] SJ
[55] Diana Whitney
[56] Sharif Abdullah
[57] NW
[58] Ken Suibielski

[59]   MH
[60]   Steven Mitchell, *A Book of Psalms* (NY: HarperCollins,
       1993), Psalm 121.
[61]   Susan Izard
[62]   David Wick
[63]   Bill Creed, S.J.

Chapter V

What Are These Not-strictly-rational Processes?

What helps me? Silence . . . worship . . . the Eucharist ... walking in nature . . . and being with folk with similar passions. . . . When we connect with people, we connect with God .[1]

In the previous chapter we saw that the Grassroots Spirituality Movement holds that we have a spark of the panentheistic one within us. If so, we can use a range of not-strictly-rational processes to help tap, foster or reveal it. What are those practices?

Introvertive Tools

As we've said, we had expected that many of our respondents would espouse meditation, contemplation, *lectio divina*, davening, and/or some form of prayer. These are the sorts of things for which spirituality is well-known. And indeed many that we spoke to do or have practiced TM, Vipassana meditation, Zen, etc., often for many years. People told us of spiritual movement practices such as Tai Chi, Chi Qong, spiritual dancing, and other forms. And indeed, virtually every person we spoke with had some such routinized "private" practices that foster "letting go." These are the sorts of practices we had expected to hear about.

For many, body work such as massage, the Alexander technique, rolfing, etc., plays an important role. One or two mentioned that part of their practice is "remembering" silence when they find themselves getting "too caught up." Indeed most remind themselves to be present when they get overly attached.

We also heard about voluntary simplicity, paring down one's life to leave room for more meaningful activities.

> *"I like to see people consuming less in their lives. Yes, voluntary simplicity. But this is important only because it is a sign that values other than materialism are operative in their lives. What I seek is not the small house but an attitude: finding something else to feed my hungry inner place."*[2]

To live content with small means,
to seek elegance rather than luxury,
and refinement rather than fashion,
to be worthy, not respectable, and wealthy, not rich,
to study hard, think quietly, act frankly,
to listen to stars and birds, babes and sages, with
open heart,
do all bravely,
await occasions,
hurry never
in a word, to let the spiritual, unbidden
    and unconscious,
grow up through the common.
This is my symphony.
            — William Ellery Channing[3]

Recently Bill Talen, who calls himself a priest of the "church of stop shopping" has been staging protests at Starbucks, toy stores, and other retail establishments. His street theatre has the intention of helping people see that shopping and buying does not bring deeper satisfaction.[4]

Extrovertive Tools

We had expected to find such introvertive processes. After all, the major spiritual traditions emphasize withdrawal from the world through monasticism, prayer, silence, asceticism, etc. Hinduism is famed for its Yoga, Buddhism for its meditation, and Taoism for its lonely sages. What we did not expect was how many of our informants regard some sort of *group process* as critical to their spiritual growth. To some this means developing and participating in some kind of group ritual: revising traditional spiritual practices to fit their more (panentheistic) theological understandings. Jews in the Jewish Renewal movement, for example, have developed prayers that acknowledge and are said to foster *ruach*, the living breath of God, as opposed to the more traditional worship of the "king of the Universe" phraseology. Others, such as the Wiccans, the Men's Movement, and others have developed dance groups, ritual communities and shamanistic primal ceremonies.[5]

But what most surprised us was the numbers of people who told us that their path included some kind of small group process.

> *"What helps me? Silence . . . worship . . . the Eucharist . . . walking in nature . . . and being with folk with similar passions. . . . When we connect with people, we connect with God."*[6]

> *"Spiritual life is both isolated and not isolated. It is not isolated because it entails a community. It is isolated in that everybody's experience of the divine is different."*[7]

Such groups play a surprisingly vital part of the grass-roots spiritual path.

"Keating's centering prayer that seeks to be in the presence helps my spiritual life a lot. But I also have a great need for being in relationship. The soul matures through mental dialogues and connections."[8]

"After I've come together with others involved with spirituality, I leave invigorated. It's like going to the community well."[9]

Some of our informants have turned to informal support groups, meeting with three or six friends with whom they could really let down their hair, to discuss personal issues. *"Good friends who understand the way I feel about things are very helpful to my spiritual life."*[10] These groups meet in the living room or coffee shop; spiritual growth over cappuccino.

To most others this meant more formal groups: sheik-led meetings of the Sufi group, ongoing "advanced" TM lectures, Zen Dharma-Talks or tea after group zazen, Bible study and / or House Church groups.

"Our [small Catholic group] has a formal structure. We come together to pray, share our lives, and explore in terms of our lives."[11]

Reformers within Judaism have created small study and support communities called *havurah* groups.

"As they prayed together, people sensed that God appeared here and now in midst of community. . . . God is found between people and other people, what Martin Buber calls Zwischen, between. God is found in relationships."[12]

The popular 12-step meetings also provide a community, some sense of commonality and the feeling of connectedness. These groups needn't be only with people from one's own school, tradition or even interests:

"Finding fellow journeyers helps on the path. Finding people who share a commitment to a journey. They may

*not even be on the same path, but finding others on a path
turns into support with working on spiritual peace.*"[13]

*"We're better off talking with one another across our tra-
ditional histories than not. We don't expect them to
believe as we do, but we're greater because of the conversation. In listening to each other we are made greater."*[14]

These groups can take some surprising shapes as well.
Our spiritually alert writing teacher, Evelyn Brush, has
structured her adult writing classes as budding spiritual
communities.[15] Their papers naturally lead into conversations about personal and spiritual issues. We also heard of
spiritual communities forming themselves around a
dance classes, healing arts classes, monthly rituals, and so
on.

Small groups, we heard, help create community and
authentic contact. They answer to the modern problem of
loneliness. "I want to work at building up my community"
was a common and oft repeated theme.

*"We don't have time for people any more. We used to
hang out on the street, but we don't now. People hunger
to make connections with others. We long to be with each
other, especially on a deeper level, where we've each made
our discoveries."*[16]

Many stressed that this personal development and community building will remain unfulfilled if they do not ultimately lead to something practical. People sought to see
communities that *do* something: feed the homeless, build
houses for the poor, give spiritual guidance to prisoners,
or engage in social action of some sort. People want to
have an impact on more than their own small worlds.

*"I want action . . . Something practical like feeding the
poor. Creating a society which works for all is a sacred
acting. Every spiritual and religious tradition leads to
the same conclusion. Working for others is the highest
form of spirituality."*[17]

Conclusions

As we will see in a later chapter, one cause of Grassroots Spirituality is that the not-strictly-rational side of life has been largely left out of the modern rational, "scientific" worldview. People long for something that fosters this more intuitive, non-linear and "messy" side of themselves. Many of the introvertive tools they are using — meditation, Tai Chi, contemplation, and other procedures — purportedly help them "let go" of rationalistic thinking. One is to let thinking go, let the mantra go, move without thought, listen for guidance, etc. These procedures are perfect answers to the desire for something besides the controlling, manipulative linearity of science and rational accounting principles.

But spiritual people have also discovered that they can get to the not-strictly-rational through a feeling-centered small group process. Things that go on in a group are often not controllable, but result from an emergent process. People share their lives on an intimate level, and intuitively explore their deepest values. These are precisely what science overlooks. People are finding deeply comforting personal contact and affirmation through their support communities. They also tell us they feel less alone on their respective "paths," and thus are able to practice their meditations or movement with greater confidence and continuity. Thus the small group process is clearly a critical addition to Grassroots Spirituality.

Finally quiet sharing in a group can sometimes lead to surprising experiences, we heard. When the stories have been told and the laughter dies down among trusting friends, we heard, we can sometimes reach a rich and delicious depth together. Stretching into the spacious openness that surrounds us all, we can sometimes find ourselves dropping into a new level, like a mutual mystical moment. Conversation at that depth can be magical.

One final note: Both the extrovertive and introvertive techniques emphasize not-strictly-rational processes. In the way Grassroots Spirituality has conceived of it, spirituality is, from the ground up, an expression of and an attempt to nourish the not-strictly-rational. "To be guided by the spirit," to "let go of expectations" or to participate in an unpredictable group are above all else hymns to what is beyond linear logic and mental control. People have turned to the more intuitive or perhaps feminine side, to that which transcends logic and understanding, to find direction and meaning. In this, the Grassroots Spirituality Movement has clearly found a response to our culture's felt dissatisfaction with science and rationality. Thus this Grassroots Movement, like every successful large scale societal movement, has found a way to address people's hurts and chafings.

Notes — Chapter V

[1]   Jeffry Steven Gaines, Executive Director, Spiritual Directors International.
[2]   Sharif Abdullah
[3]   Gary Lawless, in *Earth Prayers*, E. Roberts and E. Amidon, Eds. (San Francisco: HarperCollins, 1991).
[4]   *New York Times*, 1/1/03, Business Section, Page 1. Also see a portrait in *Utne Reader Online*.
[5]   On Wiccan rituals, see Starhawk *The Spiral Dance*. The magazine *Wingspan* is the best source for information about today's ritual-intensive men's movement.
[6]   Jeffry Steven Gaines, Executive Director, Spiritual Directors International.
[7]   Christian Peck
[8]   Charles Simpkinson
[9]   David Wick
[10] Christian Peck
[11] Susan Jorgensen
[12] Arthur Waskow
[13] Glenna Gerard
[14] Bill Creed, S.J.
[15] MPB
[16] Susan Jorgensen
[17] Sharif Abdullah's brochure.

Chapter VI

The Shape of Grassroots Spirituality

Yes, Virginia, there is a there there.

N ow, we have seen how this spirituality movement defines spirituality. And we have highlighted some of its principle causes. But we still wonder, what is this movement's shape?

Interest in spirituality is growing through a variety of schools and traditions, in a variety of contexts, under a variety of terms and guises, all over the United States and the world. It is growing within many denominations of the "churched" and in the hearts of the "unchurched." Christian women are buying inspirational spiritual books and becoming Catholic and Protestant "spiritual directors." Jewish men and women are dancing in New York and Jerusalem to Kabalistic rhythms. Men in Santa Fe are rethinking and rewriting traditional Jewish rituals on more spiritual models. Businesswomen in Rio de Janeiro are importing spiritual principles into their work places. Buddhist retreat centers in Massachusetts are sponsoring retreats for cross legged Buddhists, and Transcendental Meditators are meditating on cushions in Fairfield, Iowa and Delhi, India. A spirituality and health center is being developed in Dallas, Texas, and a magazine of that name

is now national. In Princeton, NJ, a thriving Sufi community performs healing and meditation seminars.
Lindisfarne members in England, Taizé chanters in South-
ern France, Transpersonal psychologists in Spain: it is
happening in every tradition and on every continent.

To get a picture of this wide ranging movement, keep in
mind that much of this new community has been developing *within* the various religious traditions. And there are
also many millions of the unchurched, unaffiliated, who
are also involved.

As a mesa might rise up right through state and national
boundaries, the Grassroots Spirituality Community has
risen right through traditional, new and non-traditional
boundaries. It's appeared within more spiritual wings of
every major tradition, and many minor ones. It's clearly
found in wings of Christianity, Judaism, and Islam.
Nearly every Buddhist should be counted as standing on
this mesa; so can most Transcendental Meditators. Most of
those who regularly attend Christian Mystery seminars
should be counted, though probably a smaller percentage
of those who attend mainline Protestant churches are
involved.

Then there are the many millions of the unaffiliated.
Many, not all, are clearly exploring spirituality. Many of
these folk grew up in some tradition but fell away. Some
call themselves "atheists," by which many mean, I have
discovered, "not a believer in a traditional religion" or
"not a believer in a personal God." Some got involved
with some new movement in their twenties, only to
become disaffected. Many of these experimented with lots
of other paths — so many that they can no longer identify
themselves with any one of them. Some, of course, lost
interest in the spiritual entirely. But many still very much
consider themselves seekers; this is the huge group Phil
Goldberg calls "unaffiliated seekers." They have no tradition they call "home" at this point, but they may still buy
the latest book by Deepak Chopra or Caroline Myss, will

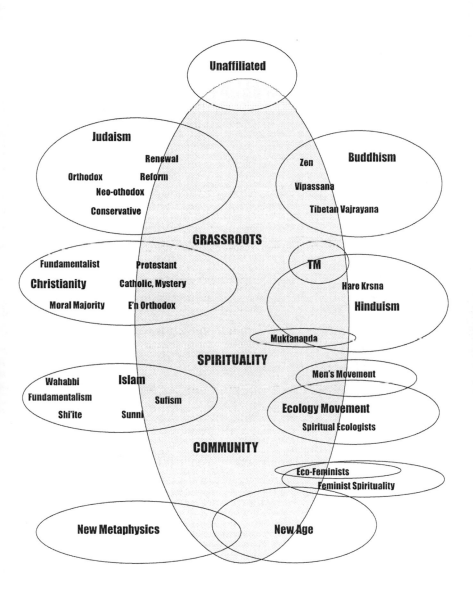

Figure 1. Venn diagram depiction of
Grassroots Spirituality

try a new seminar, and on and on. We might represent these folk with their own circle on our diagram.

Wendy Donager once suggested that we should try to define Hinduism not with a single cookie-cutter definition, but with something more like a Venn diagram. Some elements of Hinduism will espouse or practice all of the elements in the diagram, others will hold to most, others to just a few.

In fact, we should probably think of *any* large scale social movement with a Venn diagram. Take Christianity, for example. Think how many differences there are in beliefs about God, behavior, ritual or who Christ is among, say, Catholics, Russian Orthodox, evangelical Baptists, Quakers and Methodists. Religious movements, Donager suggested, are big, complicated and "messy."

Like that, let us think of this new grassroots spirituality community using a Venn diagram [see Figure 1].

What Kind of a There is There?

Does it make sense then to speak of a *single* "Grassroots Spirituality Movement?" Certainly we should not try to identify a movement of this magnitude with some single, scalpel-sharp definition. It is far too complex a human phenomenon. Those doing spirituality in health care probably share a lot with a Sufi or a Jewish Renewal participant, but they certainly do not share everything, our definition's idealized precision notwithstanding.

The point of this diagram is that despite the fact that (probably until this book) this movement as a whole hasn't had a *name*, there are millions of people in many traditions and movements that are all part of a single trans-traditional, large scale grassroots spiritual movement. We just haven't realized it yet.

A variety of traditional religions and intellectual movements have been involved in the growth of Grassroots Spirituality: Protestant openness to personal experience, the metaphysical thought of Theosophy, early twentieth century importing of Buddhist and Hindu thought, the ecological movement, the increasing acceptance of Native American spirituality — all these rivulets fed into the great ocean of Grassroots Spirituality.

The question comes up, however, just what is the relationship between the various rivulets and the ocean itself? Should we say we have only *one* grassroots movement here, or are there many individual spirituality movements that have just developed in parallel? Do we have a modern Jewish spirituality, a modern Christian spirituality, a Buddhist, Hindu, and perhaps other spirituality movements that combine several of these? If there are many discrete grassroots spirituality movements, then the patterns we observed in our interviews are just happy coincidences.

Are there many grassroots spirituality movements or one?

Another way to ask the same question: Is there is "something" here — a more or less coherent grassroots movement or is it best to say there are just changes in many ancient somethings? Is there a there there?

Old Traditions, New Boundaries

Certainly much of the growth and evolution of spirituality over the last 50 or 100 years *has* taken place within the churches, synagogues, mandirs (temples) and zendos. We might sketch the development through these strands: As Judaism becomes more reformed and its children more assimilated, Jews become more spiritual by reading Martin Buber, Abraham Heschel and Solomon Schechter. Many explored the mystical Kabala. Others formed Havruah groups, while Jewish nouveau-orthodoxy has been developing alternative, more spiritual, rituals.

Since Vatican II, Catholicism has witnessed the development of the lay spiritual directors' movement and the small church movement. New forms of spirituality have burgeoned since the vernacular became its ritual language. There has been an enormous increase of interest in Christian Hesychasm and Christian mystics like St. Theresa and Meister Eckhart. The Christian Contemplative Outreach organization teaches the contemplative prayer styles articulated by Thomas Keating and John Main.

Sufism has had resurgence in western Islam. Sufi tales and teaching stories have become popular. Sufi teachers such as Hasan Gebel and Imayyat Kahn have been very successful at bringing dikr and other forms of contemplative practices to the seeking public.

The transcendentalism developed in the nineteenth century by Emerson, Theroux and others has had its impact on American thought. Anthroposophy has continued to mature since the early twentieth, as has Theosophy. Eastern religions like Buddhism have put down vital roots in North America and Europe since they were first introduced to America at the Parliament of the World's Religions in 1893. Zen Buddhism in particular has had enormous philosophical and experiential success since they were popularized by D.T. Suzuki, Shunryo Suzuki, Baker Roshi, and Alan Watts. Hindu adherents have spread various forms of Neo-advaitan and Bhakti thought through a variety of meditation forms such as TM, ISKON (Hare Krishna), Siddha Yoga, Rajneesh, Kripalu Yoga, and the like. Such developments have been happening in all the traditions in parallel. Thus a pluralistic view — there are many parallel spiritualities — makes sense.

On the other hand, much of the vital growth of spirituality has been happening *outside* of the boundaries of the traditions. Though all have traditional forbears (who doesn't?), the most influential books — *The Road Less Traveled, Care of the Soul, The Celestine Prophecy, The Tao of Physics, A Course in Miracles,* the countless books of Ken Wilber, etc. — are not tradition-bound. Most of the most popular spiritual leaders — Caroline Myss, Larry Dossey, etc. —

emphasize that they are *not* tied to any tradition. Many of the more successful personal transformation programs — TM, est, Tai Chi, Bohmian dialogue — were largely or entirely divorced from their natal traditions. Few of these movements demand allegiance to any tradition. In fact, most say you can hold to any tradition and still participate. The more spiritual forms of psychotherapy — Transpersonal Psychology, Focusing, Hakomi therapy, Psychosynthesis, etc. — have had a huge impact on the traditional spiritualities, but are not affiliated with any religious traditions. Indeed some of these have usurped much of the traditional pastoral roles of the clergy — or the clergy have become trained in *them*. In other words, while much of the developments and interest has been *within* the traditions, a very great deal has not.

When we asked our informants about influences on their work, virtually all stated emphatically that they have learned from people and writings from a wide swath of backgrounds and traditions. Ram Dass's name came up a lot, as did that of the Dali Lama, Tich Nat Hahn, Sufis like Rumi and Rabi'a, Christians like Eckhart and Thomas Keating, Allan Watts, and on and on. The leaders of this movement to whom we spoke have also been reading each others' books.

Furthermore, *most* of our informants, both traditional clergy and those of more idiosyncratic paths, named to us a number of practices as elements of their paths. Of these TM was mentioned the most, but many count Yoga, Zen, Sufi tales, native American rituals, martial arts and other practices as pieces of their spiritual jig-saw puzzles.

It is as if the residents of the various religious houses have wandered into some huge village green to chat with each other. Then they've taken what they've learned from each other back to their respective houses, and have taught their followers what they've learned. Thus a common village-green way of being spiritual, or in this case, world-village-green viewpoint, has been slowly emerging. See below.

In short, there are forces and trends at work here that are running their courses largely independently of any one tradition, or even of all the traditions. Indeed when we looked at the movement's causes, we noted that one of the motivations for people becoming spiritual has been that many are *frustrated* with the narrowness of their churches and synagogues. No, we would be wisest to say that the development here is something bigger than any of the traditional religious institutions.

The great ocean of the spirituality movement as a whole is best understood, I believe, as a new community that is fed by many traditional rivulets, but that *includes but transcends* the traditional religious institutions. Christianity, Judaism and Islam are not responsible for, nor do they own, Grassroots Spirituality.

Of Dialects and Languages

What then has been the relationship between the rivulets of the traditions and the ocean of the Grassroots Spirituality Movement?

It is complex. Think of the development of Grassroots Spirituality as like the development of a new language — say, English. English is said to have begun in the fifth century, with the invasion of Britain by the Frisians, Saxons, Angles and Jutes. Each had their own more or less discrete language, which interacted with the indigenous Celtic.[1]

Of course, English did not magically appear the day the Saxons, Frisians and Jutes won the last battle. After their wars ended, the Frisians, Jutes, Angles, Saxons and the others settled down, farmed, married, bore children, traded, and lived their lives side by side for years and years. For many decades, no doubt, they each spoke primarily their own languages. Slowly they taught each other their words, and together developed a few common words and idioms. We can still see the same process at work in English today. It must have taken many, many decades before English began to evolve as a recognizably unified language. Think about how it must have seemed to people in those fifth or sixth centuries. If they thought about it, they probably would each have felt that that there were four or five languages on the island of Angle-land, and that those languages were largely independent of each other, but that their own language was contributing a few words to the others'. Within the first century of cohabiting on the great island, the speakers of Frisian, Angle and Saxon would probably have felt that their languages were still pretty discrete and changing in their own individuated ways, like a parallel series of independent streams.

It must have taken many years before someone could have recognized that they were all speaking roughly the same language, using material, rules, and words from each others' tongues. At some point, reflective souls could have looked around and declared, "I say, this is no longer Frisian, Jute or Angle. We seem to be jolly well speaking a new language here."

This kind of slow, organic, messy process just is the way large-scale social synergies happen. Cultures don't form major new elements overnight. But sooner or later one can say, yes, Virginia, now there *is* a there there.

This is what is happening to Grassroots Spirituality today. As we spoke with our representatives from the array of religio-spiritual "languages," we began to hear something like a single new religio-spiritual "language" being spoken. It has taken bits and pieces from the mother traditions that preceded it, but it is *not* just warmed- over Christianity, Judaism, Islam, Feminism, or nineteenth century New Thought. It has its own rules, ritual patterns and attitudes. As English did by Shakespeare's day, Grassroots Spirituality has become its own thing.

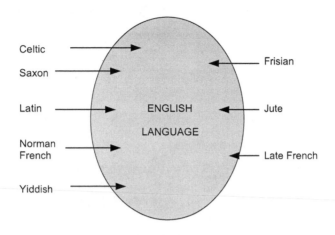

Figure 2a. Development of English

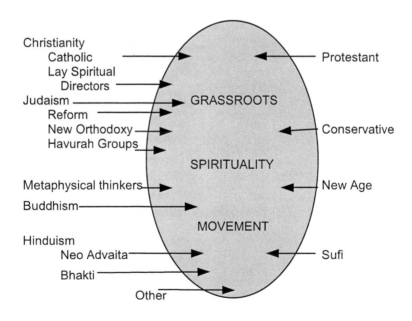

Figure 2b. Development of Grassroots Spirituality

I can well imagine that the Frisian, Angle or Saxon-speakers might claim that their language was the real "mother" of the language. Indeed it is said that because of the large influence of the Norman invaders after 1066, French speakers used to joke that English was a mere dialect of Norman French! But that would have been wrong. English soon became a discrete language of its own, neither Jute, Saxon nor French, with its own rules, patterns and vocabulary. [Figure 2a]

Grassroots Spirituality is much like that. Several more or less independent religious rivulets have fed into it. They all came with their own great wisdom and rich rituals, and have their own religious terms, assumptions, practices and jargon. And they may all see Grassroots Spirituality as primarily their tradition's own wild "offspring." But if so, they would be wrong. It is more correct to say that Grassroots Spirituality is its own thing, the bastard child of all and none of them. It drew bits and pieces from each of their genetic codes, but it now has its own code and patterns. What is there is IT'S OWN there. [Figure 2b]

Grassroots Spirituality has developed into a single spiritual "language," which has been fed by a thousand religious and philosophical streams. Each of them brought its own long and glorious history. Nevertheless, what we are witnessing is the birth of a single large Grassroots Spirituality Movement, the center of the Venn diagram, some 50–80 million Americans strong.

Once named and recognized as a single thing, as this book tries to do, it too will be seen has a more or less discrete movement, with its own peculiar, complex etiology, history, thrusts and effects.

Grassroots Movements and Dialects

As we've seen, Christians, Zen Buddhists, psychotherapists and spiritual business people all have different ways of speaking about what we're calling the "panentheistic and indwelling" ultimate. To some it is Christ Consciousness, to others Brahman, the shechinah, Buddha Mind, the Tao, chi, and so on.

It's as if the various groups are using different words, placing their emphasis on different places and rhythms. Yet all seem to be describing the same spiritual experiences, hopes, techniques, and mysteries. So how should we conceive of these differences?

Let's go back to our analogy with a language. Languages have dialects. They can sound very different. The Babu English of Bombay, the macho English of Brooklyn, the lilting Celtic English of Belfast, Bario English of Miami's little Havana, and Scottish Highland English sound very different indeed! These people may not even be able to readily understand each other. There will be many words, accents and phrases they won't share.

But if we stand back from the differences between "mon," "man" and "muun," it is clear that these folk are indeed speaking dialects of a single language. How do we know? Well, there's no simple rule. But they share a great wealth of grammar, vocabulary, linguistic structures and so on.

Like that, we should say that differences we hear in the Spirituality of female Catholics who are "defecting in place,"[2] highly concentrated Zen practitioners, and soft talking psychosynthesis counselors are something like dialects. Each school has its own expressions, stresses and emphases. Each teaches its favorite not-strictly-rational practices. Each has its own constituency. Some are centered in different geographical locales. These are something like regional "dialects" of a single sprawling movement.

In any vast social phenomena, the borders and edges are permeable. This is as true of a language as of a social movement. Think of particularly foreign dialects of English — say Welsh English, Cajun Creole English, or Jamaican Pigeon English. We might wonder if these are dialects or entirely new languages. Their grammar is more or less different, their vocabulary has many new words. At some point it will be unclear if we have a dialect or a new language. Again, the edges of vast social phenomena are always fuzzy. Perhaps we should say Cajun English or Jamaican Pigeon English are on the "margins" of the mother tongue, while Queens English or Walter Cronkite's English might represent something like the centers.

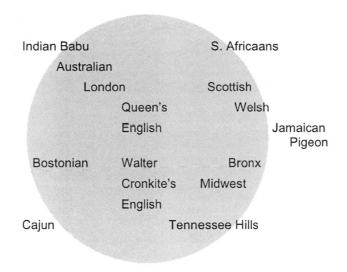

Figure 3a. English and its Dialects

The following is intended as merely a first suggestion of a Venn diagram; please do not take it as some sort of judgment.

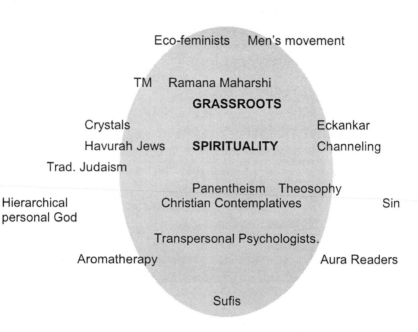

Figure 3b. Grassroots Spirituality and its "Dialects"

Some spiritual movements seem to be quite near to "the great center" of this movement. Others are clearly "dialects" of Grassroots Spirituality. Some are on the edges but still largely inside, still others seem to be on the far margins. For example, in our interviews with respected leaders from a variety of traditions, not one approvingly mentioned crystals or aromatherapy. Thus we might say advocates of these tools and techniques are on the margins of our community, a kind of minority report. A few but only a few mentioned channeling — again, margins? Almost everyone stressed the use of not-strictly-rational spiritual procedures and the hope that spirituality would guide the whole of their lives. Many mentioned meditation or contemplation approvingly. Most of those that described an ultimate typically did so with panentheistic imagery or a combination of panentheistic and personal imagery, as we saw. From our research, we should say that these tenets are near the center, the majority report, of Grassroots Spirituality.

People were quite adamant however that the understanding of the Infinite as a hierarchical, personal judging God is *not* what they're about. This then becomes outside our Venn diagram. It's like a *different* language. In fact, I believe this model serves as the center of another of the great clusters of American religious life.

This parallel between linguistic dialects and the "dialects" of Grassroots Spirituality is useful in another way. We said that most of our informants did not give us *all* of the pieces of our definition. Some no doubt simply did not get into all those pieces. Other people however espouse some but not all of the general tenets of Grassroots Spirituality. For example, a Christian Feminist might share the sense that the ultimate is not-strictly-rational and that it may be understood in a multi-cultural way. But she may combine an impersonal ultimate language with something about her personal relationship with Jesus as a guide for her. I would say she is clearly part of the Grassroots Spirituality Movement, but not strictly in its middle.

If a Jew speaks of the ultimate in panentheistic and indwelling terms, but holds that his tradition offers the *sole* authentic access to that ultimate, we might also say he is not quite bull's-eye, since the majority report recognizes a range of plausible paths. Nevertheless, he is clearly participating in this large scale social movement.

There are margins and centers here, but it is both a vague and a dynamic process. Over a lifetime, as one's opinions and attitudes change, one is likely to, in effect, move around this diagram. This is no different than is the case with any large scale social movement. Just as one's accent is likely to change as one moves from country to country, one is likely to change one's understanding of spiritual practices as one explores different pathways.

Yet despite the fact that there are no strict dogmas, no sign up sheets, no catechisms, no sharp boundaries, no litmus tests, there *is* a movement here. Let us not fall into the trap of saying that because its edges are fuzzy, there is no such thing as "English." Rather we should say that this is a huge and complicated social entity, and its borders are necessarily fuzzy. It may be a vague and complex movement, like any widespread language or any large scale social phenomenon. Nonetheless, though messy, it is one.

Yes, Virginia, there is a there there.

Village Greens and Outlying Homes

Our story, however, does not end with the various "dialects." And this is one more reason we should say that we have *one* spirituality movement, not many. Quite a few of our informants told us that over the years they have read from or practiced techniques from other traditions. Catholic Father Thomas Keating, who helped develop Christian Contemplative Prayer, is said to have learned the Hindu derived Transcendental Meditation technique. Christian Robert Jonas, director of the Empty Bell in Watertown, Mass., has integrated Zen Buddhist practices into his Christian teachings. Sufi Suhrawardi Gebel learned practices from a variety of traditions. Christians have read Buddhists, Buddhists, who often began as Jews, have read Christian texts, and Jews like Sarah Rabinowitz began with Eastern meditation practices.[3] Leaders and practitioners from the full array of traditions are quite cognizant of the burgeoning interest in spirituality, have attended a variety of seminars, and have learned a great deal of what leaders from other traditions and schools are teaching.

As a result, the traditions themselves are moving in more spiritual directions. As Jews come through the doors of the synagogues, looking for spiritual tools and guidance, their Rabbis and counselors face the choice of satisfying their interests or losing them. Thus their institutions are developing or reshaping processes, rituals and techniques to answer their constituents' felt-needs. They know if they don't satisfy the inner cravings, they will lose their adherents. Thus traditional Jews are "rediscovering" their meditation tradition, mainline Christian churches are "re-emphasizing" their contemplative "roots," and so on.[4]

Just as English words like "telephone," "parking," "weekend," and "shopping" have found their way back into French, one of the shaping languages of English, it is as if the common village-green "language" of Grassroots Spirituality is flowing back into the various tongues from which it sprang.

Let's think about this image of a village green with homes around it.[5] In the community green, people meet one another on walks and park benches. They swap stories, hear each other's thoughts, words and phrases and discuss things. They develop more or less common sets of beliefs, attitudes and assumptions. They then return back to their homes, and relate back, now within the vocabulary they have developed over the years with their loved ones, the new things that they have been hearing. It's a very natural back and forth process.

Like that, the common discussions attitudes and important books of the Grassroots Spirituality movement are feeding attitudes, understandings, and techniques back to the home traditions, and slowly changing them. When they change, of course, they retain much of their traditional vocabulary. But the old wineskins are now being filled with a new kind of wine. [See figure 4, below.]

The arrows of influence point both ways. Each tradition, as we have noted, has contributed thoughts, vocabulary, tools and resources to the Grassroots Spirituality community. In turn, The Grassroots Spirituality Movement feeds its set of attitudes, insights, and techniques back to the traditions. Zen-like and TM-like meditation practices are now regulars in Christian convents; spiritual healing has found its way into hospital operating rooms; and Eastern

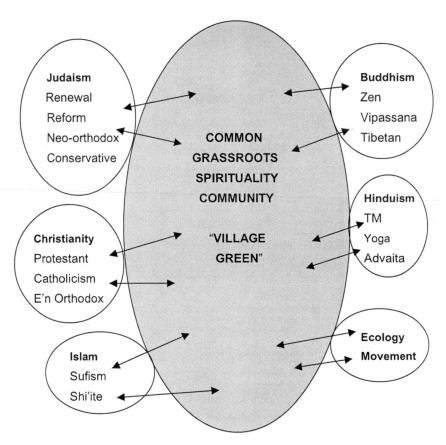

Figure 4. Village Green Model of Spiritual Communities

notions of enlightenment are now being applied to western mystics.[6] The mother shapes the child. And as he grows up, the child influences his mom. What could be more natural?

But do not misunderstand this. There *is* a village green sensibility. Despite the fact that the different homes hear and translate that mentality somewhat differently, we can and should say that on the green there is a there there.

The Perennial and the Novel

After writing up our definition of spirituality, I realized that what we heard again and again is quite similar to what has come to be known as the "perennial philosophy." This term, coined by Leibniz, was popularized by Aldous Huxley. Huxley tells us,

"The *Philosophia Perennis* [is] the metaphysic that recognizes a divine Reality substantial to the world of things and lives and minds; the psychology that finds in the soul something similar to, or even identical with, divine Reality; the ethic that places man's final end in the knowledge of the immanent and transcendent Ground of all being."[7]

According to Huxley and other authors, the perennial philosophy is the common set of thoughts and attitudes that are found in a wide range of the world's traditions, especially "primitive peoples," and in esoteric strands within the major world traditions.

Both Grassroots Spirituality and the perennial philosophy assert something like an indwelling panentheistic ultimate. Huxley calls this the "immanent–transcendent One, the essence and principle of all existence" which is the ground of all existence.[8] This infinite One can be found at the inmost level of the soul, says Huxley: That thou art. "The God within and God without . . . cannot be realized and experienced except in the deepest and most central part of the soul."[9] This, he says is "ineffable in terms of discursive thought," which is reminiscent of our informants' stress on the not-strictly rational.[10]

It is right to say that the attitudes and beliefs of the Grassroots Spirituality Movement are deeply congruent with the perennial philosophy, strands of which are found in the esoteric schools in the great religious systems. This is not too surprising, for many of the leading authors and teachers of Grassroots Spirituality read and refer back to

the perennialist thinkers like Eckhart, Shankara,
Vipassana Buddhist teachers, Blake, etc., and even Huxley
himself!*

But make no mistake: Grassroots Spirituality is something quite new in human history. The following features
distinguish it from *any previous* school or philosophy.

Scale. In general, the esoteric strands in the traditions that
Huxley calls perennial have remained the minority.
Advaita Hinduism, Prajnaparamita Buddhism, mystical
Christianity, the Kabala, etc. were all important but
minority voices within their traditions. Generally a more
theistic, personalistic, mythological, security-centered
religion dominated: "Oh Lord, please make the rain come .
. . make the smallpox go away . . . bring Grandma back to
health" were the kind of cries one was more likely to hear
on the streets of Banaras, Jerusalem, Medina or Lourdes
than was "That art Thou." The panentheistic viewpoint
has never before been the report of such a majority.

Until now. If Ray's, Barna's, Gallup's, and Zinnbauer's
findings are correct, then someplace between 50 and 84
million people in America alone are moving in a spiritual
direction. If we count the fairly open minded seekers sitting in the church and synagogue pews, as we should, this
movement is probably well more than half of America.
There has *never*, to my knowledge, been such a mass spiritual movement.

Indeed, the perennial voice has generally been confined
to the monasteries, convents and secret (esoteric) schools
of the traditions. The walls of monastic cells were erected
around such teachings. Ostensibly these walls were to
protect the teachings and the practitioners, and offer them

* This is not to say that Huxley was the *cause* of the Grassroots
Spirituality movement. The causes are legion, and far more complex (and interesting) than any one figure. But he is often read,
and probably was having similar experiences and insights as
many of our subjects.

to souls that were well educated, literate and spiritually prepared. But those same walls also kept these teachings from the outside world. That is, they protected the ordinary believers and the ecclesiastical and governmental powers from the anti- hierarchical implications of these teachings. As we've noted, panentheism challenges the mediating role of priests, bishops, popes, rabbis and mullahs. It also challenges the old rationale that kings have a divine right to rule. These were powerful if unconscious reasons to lock such dangerous teachings behind monastic doors.

But now kings no longer rule by divine right, and the church hierarchy has lost much of its sway, especially in the recent Catholic Church. As those hierarchies have lost sway, and masses have learned to contemplate in their living rooms, these teachings have touched hearts on a scale never seen before. If you add up every soul before 1850 who had ever even heard of a transcendent–immanent ultimate by any name, I doubt it would be more than a tiny fraction of today's 50–80 million. There are probably more panentheists alive today than there have been in all of human history!

The ramifications of this fact are nearly unfathomable. Humanity will be shaped by the after-shocks of such a tectonic theological shift for centuries. So far, the effect on our polity and work lives has offered us mere hints. But when this really sinks in (as these things generally do in time), when we finally shift our world view and our ways of acting in alignment with this new sense of what it is to be human, who knows what changes are in store for human civilization?

Middle Class. Most previous explorations of these matters has been confined largely to the monks, religious specialists, and other subgroups that were supported by their communities enough to spend the bulk of their time in such explorations. Our findings are that the Grassroots

Spirituality Movement has arisen in the United States primarily among an urban, educated, middle or upper middle class populace. The widespread financial comfort and education of this populace have shaped this movement. Unlike any previous spirituality movement, meditation, reading and writing of spiritual texts are now in the hands of a widely educated audience with both the leisure to meditate and attend retreats, but who also work, raise children, etc.

As a result, Grassroots Spirituality folks have begun to explore, in a way never before seen, how to be spiritual in the workplace, how to raise children spiritually, and other practical matters. From the spirituality of changing diapers, to "Everyday Zen" to the spirituality of marriages to *Zen and the Art of Motorcycle Maintenance*, folks in this Grassroots Spirituality world have been exploring how to deal with everyday life from a spiritual perspective. This gives Grassroots Spirituality a practical edge never before seen in any perennialist school. No monk or nun could have written Thomas Moore's *Soul Mates*, about relationships, Joko Beck's *Everyday Sacred*, or Ken Wilber's *Sex, Ecology and Spirituality*. These and other books like them could only have been written in today's more complicated context.

Psychologized, medicalized. The Perennial Philosophies were developed in a variety of traditions throughout history. Virtually all of Huxley's references were to texts written before either psychology or modern medicine. Grassroots Spirituality appears well after Freud's discovery that there are relationships between childhood experiences, dreams, fantasies, and the maturation process, and after we learned that penicillin cures infections. Thus this movement has had to integrate psychological and medical systems with spiritual concerns. Caroline Myss, for example, has attempted to weave Kundalini, chakras, medicine and psychology into a single intuitive typology. Scott Peck and Thomas Moore are both trained psychologists. Deepak Chopra is an MD. Recently authors like Larry Dossey, Herbert Benson and Keith Wallace have attempted to scientifically verify the effects of meditation, prayer and other spiritual practices. This has given the Grassroots Spirituality Movement a set of scientific and psychological issues to grapple with that are unlike all previous incarnations of perennialism.

Henotheism. Previous perennialist schools knew of many other such schools. Shankara, who is credited with developing Advaita Hinduism, no doubt knew of Buddhism and possibly Jainism, but certainly nothing of Christianity, Taoism, or Kabala. Eckhart knew of some Sufis, but no Taoists, Jains or Sikhs. But today leaders of any of these traditions know of the existence of all the others, and most, we have seen, recognize that there are many plausible ways to speak of and move towards the Infinite. In ways great and small, we are quite comfortable with the fact that there are many ways to speak of and attain the One. Even though advocates may regard their way of speaking of the panentheistic ultimate as true, Grassroots Spirituality's constituents are generally comfortable with the thought that there are other perfectly valid ways to speak of the infinite. Technically then, we are all functionally *henotheists*. That is, we all hold our version of the infinite to be ultimate without denying the ultimacy of other systems. In the face of real knowledge and respect for other traditions, this movement has a more open minded stance than any previous perennialist schools, which, for all their wisdom, tended to subtly present their own way as superior.

Individualistic. Western society is famously individualistic. Having lost much of our social and communal groundings, our extended families and our village self-definitions, we have become communities of individuals. Each of us charts our own course, which is often quite different from our parents. As a result, many of us have combined traditions, spiritual philosophies and practices in our own idiosyncratic ways. Some of us have prayed, gone to healers and gotten Rolfed. Others of us have practiced meditation, spiritually oriented psycho-therapy, traveled on pilgrimages, and so on. We each forge our own pathways towards grace.

This lends the Grassroots Spirituality Movement a pre-viously unimaginable range of choices. Each of us must now choose from a cornucopia of paths and masters, and combine them in our own idiosyncratic ways. The benefit of this is that we can tailor make our pathways to our per-ceived needs: designer Gods as a recent *Utne Reader* put it. The drawback, as many of our informants have lamented, is that we tend to be lonely on our paths.

Marketed. The multiplication of choices lends this move-ment a market driven character also never seen before. Whereas a Hesychast, Zen or Hasid master could simply dictate practices to their largely unquestioning devotees, today's spiritual guides effectively must compete for dis-ciples, for the broad intellectual marketplace, and for adherents' time. Because potential students are picking and choosing their way among the whole panoply of spiri-tual options, today's teachers find themselves driven to write clearly and appealingly, market themselves well, do PR for their groups, become "media savvy," and become showmen and women of the spirit. Meditation, healing and even prayer, once (purportedly) the free gift from heart to heart, is sold, marketed and copyrighted.

As a result, spirituality has been hucksterized, if you will, and in the eyes of many, cheapened. What was once the free stairway to infinite life now appears just another stairway to somebody's wealth. And we are all suspicious.

Nonetheless such mass marketing has helped make spirituality accessible to people on unheard-of scales. Millions of copies of *The Celestine Prophecy*, of the *Chicken Soup for the Soul* series, and of *Be Here Now* have meant that spirituality may be having an effect on society's thought and behavior never before imaginable.

Notes — Chapter VI

[1]   The language later took on the influences of German, priestly Christianity (with words like angel, martyr, psalm), early Danish (after the Viking invasion in 793), and of course Norman French, after 1066, from whom Latinate terms entered the lexicon (words like government, administration, jurisprudence, soverign) and brought English a greater capacity to express subtle distinctions.

[2]   *Defecting in Place: Women Claiming Responsibility for Their Own Spiritual Lives,* by Miriam Therese Winter, Adair Lummis and Allison Stokes (New York: Crossroad, 1995).

[3]   Probably the most famous such interchange was the widely publicized meeting between Jewish leaders and the Dalai Lama. See *The Jew and the Lotus.*

[4]   Do not get me wrong. I am not saying those contemplative roots are not there. Many "roots" are there. The point is that it is *this* strand of roots that they are motivated to rediscover. For the substance of this paragraph, I am indebted to Tamar Frankiel.

[5]   I first heard this from Catherine Albanise.

[6]   Zen is being practiced in an Episcopalian convent in Mendham, NJ; Julie Mott is doing healing in operating theatres; as for "enlightenment," for which there is no equivalent term in the West, see John White, *What is Enlightenment* (Los Angeles, Jeremy P. Tarcher, 1984), pp. 12–129.

[7]   Aldous Huxley, *The Perennial Philosophy* (NY: Harper Colophon, 1945), p. vii.

[8]   Huxley, p. 22.

[9]   Huxley, p. 2.

[10] Huxley, p. 21.

Chapter VII

The Causes of Grassroots Spirituality

Where pain is felt or feared, and normal means of mastery seem inadequate, there [religion or spirituality] comes into play . . . [Such movements focus] upon sore spots, upon tense areas where people chafe and worry, scarcely able to cope.

Norvin Hein

Sociologists and scholars of religion say that large social movements are generally "over-determined." By that they mean that they have many varied, loosely intersecting yet redundant causes, any one of which potentially could cause the movement. The civil rights movement, for example, was probably caused by such intersecting elements as increasing education for African Americans, a slowly rising standard of living in the face of a large racial gap in income, racial integration of the Army during World War II, the new power of radio and television to broadcast images of white wealth and later police brutality, the effectiveness of Gandhi's non-violent strategies in the 30s and 40s, the creativity and charisma of Martin Luther King and other African American leaders, developing ideas about equality, and so on. Any and all of these helped give birth to that movement. It was "over-determined."

The Grassroots Spirituality Movement is even larger. It also is no doubt over-determined. Thus in the following let us not argue over which is the one critical cause. Rather let us identify some of its principle causes.

Demographic Shifts: Rural, Urban, Exurban

As Norvin Hein says, religious or spiritual systems generally emerge as a way of addressing people where they hurt, chafe or worry, and where ordinary means cannot alleviate that chafing. Thus, for example, on a Hurricane Island, people probably worry a lot about hurricanes, yet cannot protect their children or roofs from the winds. If so, they will be likely to assuage their worries with prayers to the hurricane god.

A corollary of this: when a people undergo a large scale, long term shift in their social situation, their hurts and worries will be likely to change. If a social group finds itself living for a century or two under a new set of circumstances, their worries and hurts are likely to change. If so, their religious or spiritual systems will be likely to change to address their new concerns. To continue our example, if the Hurricane Islanders moved off the island to the mainland plains, they would be unlikely to actively worry about hurricanes. Instead they might find themselves anxious about starvation or drought or the tribe across the mountains. If their religion or spiritual system is to keep working for them, it will have to change to address their new fears and hurts.

Religious systems do not shift to respond to short term changes. We were and are unlikely to see major religious shifts as a response to something like the September 11th attacks, the tragic death of John F. Kennedy or Sputnik. These are the kinds of things temporal institutions and leaders must address, however successfully. Rather religious or spiritual systems tend to change when a large group of people undergo shifts in their situation for many decades or centuries, like moving from farms to cities, nomadic lives to farming, or the like. Global warming, if it effects enough lives for a long enough time, might be the kind of thing a religious or spiritual system would have to address. But it would do so slowly and in deep ways.

During the last century Western society has witnessed enormous social, demographic and conceptual shifts. Whereas 150 years ago roughly three quarters of Americans lived on farms or in small rural villages, today more than three quarters live in or near cities. In modern cities, we live near people from other countries, lineages and places, and whom we may not even know. Often we are afraid of them, for they seem different. At work we find ourselves next to people from other lands and backgrounds, and who often have very different habits and beliefs. We seldom share, or even discuss, our deep values with our workmates or our neighbors. We probably do not know their children. Most of us no longer work with people from our neighborhoods.

Cities themselves have changed too. Whereas once urban neighborhoods were centers of ethnic heritage, customs, shops, art, and often languages, providing a sense of community, today such coherent ethnic communities are being challenged. In Los Angeles, Chicago, Paris or New York City, for example, people of Indian, Korean, African, Jewish, European, Hispanic, or Vietnamese descent live and work side by side.

Recently we have witnessed the growth of what is sometimes called the "exurban" setting, in which people live in relatively anonymous suburbs, and telecommute from houses or other non-urban settings. Here again, we are facing a shift away from intact communities, even the relatively superficial and transient "community" of the office.

With the invention of automobiles, airplanes, and boats, we have become ever more mobile. According to the Census Bureau, 19–20 per cent of Americans move every year.[1] Sociologist Mary Pipher finds that 72 per cent of Americans don't know their neighbors.[2] Few of us live in our natal city or, often, country. We modern humans have lost our once-natural village and communal connections, and at some deep level this hurts.

Even our jobs are shifting. According to one estimate, 25% of today's jobs had not even been invented 10 years ago!

We are wealthier as a society than we were 150 years ago. Only a small minority are truly worried about putting food on the table or having a roof over their heads. Few of us are concerned with basic material survival from like draught or starvation. (Really, do you personally know *anyone* who actively wonders where their next drink of water will come from?) Nor, with our reasonably stable legal systems, modern police forces and armies, are most of us actively worried about overall safety or basic security issues (the recent fears generated by a handful of terrorists notwithstanding). However, real fear of the hordes across the way was indeed one of the concerns of people in lawless steppes. Such matters of "basic survival" are not really where most Americans hurt.

But we do worry. Our recurring worries have more to do with alienation and aloneness. We often feel alone, lost in an anonymous and meaningless world, cut off. We moderns, largely comfortable and safe, often struggle with feeling like we're on a mouse wheel, with superficial connections, our lives lacking long term significance. We fear that we lack deep roots. Exacerbating this, many of us have lost our stable nuclear families, lost our routinized contact with extended families, lost our solid church and neighborhood communities, and, with the rise of suburbs, even lost our ethnic urban communities. Unlike 150 years ago, most of us do not share a life-history with our neighbors or the people we work with.

In sum, one of the deepest pains of our civilization has to do with a widespread sense of lostness, alienation, and aloneness. As Robert Wuthnow puts this:

> "Ours is a highly fluid society. Many of us lead anonymous lives. We no longer live in the same neighborhoods all our lives or retain close ties with our kin. [Spirituality] is clearly rooted in the breakdown of these traditional support structures and in our continuing desire for community."[3]

People in modern times, as Durkheim and others have often pointed out, commonly struggle with alienation, anomie and meaninglessness. Some of our interviewees saw this:

> *"People are hungry for connections because our society is so disconnected. Heart to heart connections are so rare."*[4]

> *"What's missing in modern life is the sense of belongingness. We all long for the feeling that others share our lives and struggles with us."*[5]

Grassroots Spirituality, which as we have seen is a largely urban, middle class and suburban phenomenon, is rising in part to address some of the pain of alienation that arises out of these fundamental demographic shifts. Many traditional religious institutions were oriented around providing a sense of security and safety in a dangerous world, in which starvation and drought were common worries. They also grew out of villages and shtetles which had steady constituencies and families. Alienation and aloneness were not these peoples' worries.

But they *are* ours. And Grassroots Spirituality is one way to address them. It offers a sense of connection with something that seems true, deep and ultimate. It responds well to the craving for stability, depth and meaning.

In relatively stable and intact communities, like villages or ethnic urban pockets, religious systems can serve the function of legitimating the community's social patterns and assumptions. Thus traditional churches articulated deep rationales for sexual, economic and social mores.

But in our times, we each have the privilege of determining where we live and our sexual and life-style orientations. So it makes sense that our spirituality should be utterly portable. We can carry our mantras or our favorite prayers with us from city to city, toting our yoga mats and our direct experiences with us no matter where or how often we move. We can meditate or pray whether we are gay, straight, bi, button down or going back to the farm. Our sense of deep connection to the spiritual infinite goes with us, even if we've utterly lost any steady social connections. The craving for a sense of connection is particularly evident in those who have adapted traditional Native American imagery that only spoke of connection to a particular place or mountain (use of which would be patently ridiculous in our mobile lives). Now they speak instead of our connection to "the Earth."

Spirituality often centers on practices one might do alone. But meditating on a lonely cushion does not satisfy our natural craving for human connection. It is not surprising then that in addition to meditative and other introvertive practices, we see in the Grassroots Spirituality Movement an emphasis on small groups, quiet human connections, and community- building. The same theme is evident when people seek a sense of connection with nature, other species or the ecosystem. Finally in its integration of diverse views and traditions, including philosophies from both East and West, Grassroots Spirituality may be seen as working towards addressing our modern sense of fragmentation.

Changes in Gender Roles, Family Structures, and Rise of the Feminine

Due to a variety of technological, economic, demographic and other factors that we needn't explore here, the last half century witnessed unmistakable changes in gender roles and new and more open attitudes towards sexuality. New family structures, more diverse sexual options, the ability to have sex without risking pregnancy, and new social attitudes have led to greater choices and roles for women.

Many of our informants observed that part of the reason for the rise of Grassroots Spirituality has to do with the rise of the feminine voice and sensibility. Interest in female goddess figures and the female side of God (Sophia, Mary, Shechinah) is growing. An increasing number of women are leading and participating in spiritual activities (Angeles Arrien, Frances Vaughan, Gurumayi, Gangaji, Caroline Myss, Mother Theresa, Charlotte Joko Beck, Pema Chodrin, etc.). Even more important, roughly 66% of the participants in small spiritual groups are women.[6]

But the most important influence here, according to many informants, is subtler. In Grassroots Spirituality's tone and style — its emphasis on relationship, human contact, exploration and interpersonal support — the spiritual world is now highly shaped by a feminine sensibility. We see this influence in spirituality's emphasis on inclusion, that which indwells, and on the intuitive. Grassroots Spirituality also emphasizes the healing power of intimate relationships, especially those of small groups.

Baby Boomers and 60s Revolutionaries

Many of our informants observed that the current interest in spirituality is in part an inheritance of the sixties. They said that the interest in spirituality is the outgrowth of the *"countercultural revolution of the 1960s . . . when psychedelic drugs opened doors of perception."*[7] Wade Clark Roof's researches suggest that the people who are highly involved with Grassroots Spirituality today tend to be those who were deeply influenced by the sixties counterculture.[8]

During the sixties and early seventies, many young people questioned reality, and opened their worldviews to broader possibilities of experience, be they new Eastern philosophies worlds or drug-induced inner worlds. Psychology came into its own during this period, and it became possible to talk of the nature of human motivations and experiences in ways other than the strictly rational.

The sixties also articulated a disillusionment with existing institutions, especially the churches and synagogues, that were perceived to be on the wrong side of civil rights and of Vietnam.

This opened the door to the enormous interest in new religions. It was a time in which barriers about gender roles, sexual practices, and mindsets were broken down through drugs and other techniques. It was also the time of breaking down the assumptions of the establishment and of challenging authority in general. But as people have matured and begun building their careers, some of this spiritual zeal cooled.

As one of our informants put it, the sixties may be viewed as a period of "breaking down." But after the "breaking down," the more difficult "constructive" challenge has been percolating ever since. Chastened, aged and refined by the meditative practices and spiritual disciplines, people are now attempting to reshape their lives and institutions in the light of those youthful discoveries, applying their hard-won inner insights in more sophisticated ways.

> *"We've seen what's wrong with the old ways. We've learned how to meditate and free ourselves from our sexual constrictions and be more authentic towards each other through therapy. But now we are asking, how are we going to apply this in practice?"*[9]

Indeed there is more *responsible* spiritual activism today than ever before. Witness the mature efforts of the Fetzer

Foundation, the Institute of Noetic Sciences, the Forge Institute, the Templeton Foundation, the Trinity Institute, and The United Religions Initiative. We are witnessing a burbling of attempts to forge new spiritual or religious systems with more mature skills. New rituals, ideas of religion, theological systems, institutions, and spiritual experiences are now being integrated with more savvy organizational work and market research.

In other words, Grassroots Spirituality may represent the maturation of the naive, zealous spirituality of the sixties. Just as the gender revolution represents the maturation of bra-burning feminism, so too mature Grassroots Spirituality, with its attempt to integrate well-grounded spiritual principles into our society and institutions, represents the maturation of the guru movements. In this way, the 60s served as a catalyst for today's more mature explorations. *"We're all grown up now, and we're trying to do it right this time."*[10]

Grassroots Spirituality expresses the maturing of the baby boomer generation in another way. Many boomers never stopped their spiritual practices. Many of the folks we spoke with have never missed a day of meditation or prayer in 20 or 30 years. And many of them have by now risen to positions of leadership: Pema Chodrin, Gangaji, Rabbi Larry Kushner, Ken Wilber, Arthur Waskow, Jack Kornfield, Harvey Aronson, Martin Rutte, Frances Vaughan, Roger Walsh, and many others have continued on their respective paths for decades and are now mature leaders in their own right. This status has allowed them to speak up. *"No longer the lieutenants of some shyster gurus, many of this generation are now the leaders. They are saying now I'm ready to enact this vision responsibly."*[11]

On the other hand, it would be easy to *over*estimate the importance of the sixties. J. Gordon Melton points out that, contrary to popular belief, the mushrooming of new religions actually began in the 1950s, the decade *before* the sixties. Whereas before 1950 an average of 35 new religions were formed each decade, in the 50s that number shot up two and a half times, to some 88, and doubled again in the sixties.[12] This suggests that the sixties were a *symptom* of a deeper and more long term demographic shift and its correlative shift in deep religious needs. Though the exciting counterculture era got the press, it may have been a symptom of something deeper.

ABC: Anything But the Church

Many of our spiritual informants reported feeling disaffected from our large scale institutions. It was a leitmotif: over and over we heard that the corporations, governments and especially the churches "have let us down."

> *"I was turned off by the more institutional approaches. There is judgment there on all sorts of levels."*[13]

> *"Institutions are not satisfying the hunger . . . people are finding social things, programmatic things, but not much to satisfy the spiritual ache."*[14]

Religiously, the deepest disappointment was clearly with the churches and synagogues. This has only been exacerbated by the Catholic Church's pedophile scandals. People are drawn elsewhere, or, as professor of religion Stuart Smithers put this, ABC, Anything But the Churches.[15]

In what is possibly an overstatement, one professor said, "*the churches as custodians of truth are pretty much irrelevant today for the overwhelming majority of people in our society.*"[16] Their moral or political proclamations no longer hold the automatic allegiance of even their congregants; they are one voice among many.

Several of our interviewees told us that even as teens they felt that the old "religious formulas, the pictures of the spiritual life" were just not working. Many noted this: the idea that giving money to the church or synagogue could somehow do something for our spiritual connections came to seem absurd.

"I grew up Jewish and was moderately satisfied with my religion. But something told me this is just not enough. We're just collecting money to save the Russian Jews, or to help Israel, or some other Jewish cause. I wondered, what kind of religious life is this? Even before I knew about things Eastern, there was something about this whole direction that said, this is just not enough."[17]

Similarly, the idea that "not sleeping with my boyfriend would make some distant God happy" just seemed like repressive nonsense.

"Even Catholics are now willing to talk of sex now as non-sinful. We share an awareness that we are sexual beings and that sex can even be holy. This is, of course, connected with the change in our larger culture."[18]

How did the churches and synagogues fail? In part, their difficulties are probably the result of the kind of changing demographics and circumstances that we described earlier. People used to be Presbyterians, Jews or Catholics largely because their parents were. They went to some particular church or temple largely because their great grandparents had settled near others in their ethnic groups and their parents prayed there. It was only natural that people should pray along with their forebears. But as we have become more mobile, it is no longer inevitable that we will choose our parents' church or synagogue, or even live near it. Those old familiar haunts have lost their inevitability as the places for our search for the Infinite.

Frankly, one of the most often mentioned reasons the churches in particular have lost sway is sex. As these largely male-led institutions became so obsessed with sex, gender and reproductive issues, they lost many of their more open- minded constituents. From its emphasis on sexual abstinence, avoiding birth control, the "evils" of pre-marital sex, as well as its homophobia, the Catholic church was frequently singled out as the most patriarchal, repressive, and out-of-touch ecclesiastical institution. Yet *all* the churches, we heard from our (frequently disaffiliated) Grassroots respondents, have gotten bogged down in such matters.

The problem however is broader than mere sexual mores. The churches began, several observed, as instigators of rich traditions. But over the centuries they have become the *guardians* of those same traditions, and of their own considerable financial and political power. They often are seen as conservative, even regressive, social institutions, and have become ill-suited to respond to the fast moving changes of our social context, demographics, life styles and meaning-systems. These text-based, catechism-bound, slow-moving traditions just cannot keep up, our respondents felt. One pastoral Councilor puts this well:

> *"It was the church's job to preserve the tradition that gave them life and authority. The churche's role has been to hold on to the tradition, to preserve. But I think they've held on at the expense of themselves not evolving. As a result, the institutions have become burdensome to growing people and are not empowering people."* [19]

On the other hand, Grassroots Spirituality, with its vague, internal orientation and utter malleability, is more able to respond flexibly to our new needs for religiosity.

We must not point the fingers of blame solely at the churches and synagogues though. They are themselves merely players in a larger societal drama. Jack Healey, a spiritually sensitive, faithful Catholic, points out that what is really driving the rectory is the needs of its constituents: many faithful parents want to raise their children in a stable Catholic lifestyle. It is familiar to them like a well-worn jacket, and they want to bequeath its safe, warm and predictable security to their children. Whatever the reason, these mothers and fathers are in effect saying to the priests, "*I want you to raise my child, and teach them in just the way I grew up. I want that stability for my child.*"[20] These needs, Healey notes, serve as a powerful force to keep things from changing. Thus the conservatism of the churches and their parochial schools play important protective role in this Catholic family sub-culture's search for stability and old time values. But that role is in conflict with the longings of other groups.

On the other hand, the churches themselves certainly bear some of the responsibility for their failure to recognize that their "distant, judging God" theology is no longer working for many. But they have been unable to come up with a more plausible and satisfying religious model.

Fritjof Capra suggests in *The Turning Point* that this new modern worldview owes much to modern physics, which says that all of reality is part of a larger continuum, the "quantum vacuum state." Modernity's new worldview also is reflected by our new sense of ecological connectedness. We conceive of our universe and of the planet as interconnected. In this continuum, there is no place for a distant father-God who is "out there" someplace, and who judges our actions from some distant heavenly realm. Furthermore, with our increasingly autonomous sense of ourselves, and with our increasingly sophisticated view of our own psychological abilities, we may no longer sense a reason for some mediating figure or some powerful holy other to magically raise us to sanity and happiness. In the face of these changing views, our needs and self-images have changed. And few churches have successfully responded.

Whatever the reasons for its failures, the Grassroots Spirituality Movement has risen in part because there is a whole constituency — perhaps the "cultural creatives" — which is not averse to change and experimentation.[21] And when this openness is combined with a feeling that the churches and synagogues have let them down, a whole new spiritual experimentation and direction has been the inevitable result.

What goes for the churches goes as well for corporations and governments. Several mentioned to us that people used to feel that they could count on their corporate employer for meaning in their lives. "I am an IBM manager" used to mean security and identity. But since the era of downsizing, notes business consultant Martin Rutte, people can no longer count on their corporations, and so they have looked to something more permanent for meaning and orientation.[22] Thus the silver lining of downsizing, says Rutte, may be that people are turning to something of more ultimate value.

The Smorgasbord Effect

There has never before been an era in which every single major religious tradition is readily available to any educated person. On the shelves of every major bookstore can be founds hundreds of hearty, thoughtful books on every major religion and spiritual school: Buddhism, Advaita Hinduism, esoteric and exoteric Christianity, philosophical and alchemical Taoism, holographic models of spirituality, Meister Eckhart's desert spirituality,[23] Nagarjuna's *shunyata*, emptiness, and on and on. Since the 1960s, courses in every major religion (and many minor ones) have been offered at nearly every college nationwide.

Virtually every major American city is now home to a cornucopia of churches, temples, synagogues, mosques, storefront Tai Chi centers, Taoist monasteries, and Buddhist Viharas. Rituals can be enjoyed any day of the week in Latin, Hebrew, Sanskrit, Swahili, Pali, Arabic, and even English.

We each confront — for the first time in history — the world's *smorgasbord* of religions, about which we all read, and from which we all must choose.

This smorgasbord of options, notes sociologist Nancy Ammerman, has been exacerbated by a little noticed change in America's immigration policy. In 1965, quotas favoring Europeans were shifted, and it became easier for many Asians and other non-Europeans to immigrate to America.[24] With the new influx of both lay and priestly Vietnamese, Burmese, Chinese Buddhists, and Hindus, the overall stew of religions in this country thickened. Some of the new religious leaders — Tich Nat Hanh, Rajneesh, Prabavananda, Trogyam Rimpoche, and others — have played an enormous part in making their respective traditions both more accessible and acceptable. In addition, non-European adherents of Christianity have changed and are changing the face of American Christianity towards other viewpoints. These facts are in turn part of the immense diffusion and intermingling of religions old and new around the world. This in turn was the inevitable consequence of modern transportation and communication technologies and newly won political openness.[25]

But in part as a result, every educated American, indeed every Westerner, now faces a cacophony of religious options and choices. If they have been relatively open-minded and diligent, they have probably explored many. This has been exacerbated by the explosion of intermarriages. We are now far more likely than our parents to have explored other religions, read about other traditions, and even converted. Americans are now likely to be in a denomination *other* than their parents, and very possibly in an altogether different religion. This is especially true for the urban, mobile, educated section of America from which Grassroots Spirituality has emerged.

"I think of my Jewish parents as the first generation in this process. They've hardly ever been to a church. But I have had bishops and Muslims as friends."[26]

As part of our interviews we asked many of our respondents to identify their "religion." Much to our surprise, when we asked that question, most just laughed out loud! It turns out that by far the dominant category of our spiritual respondents, as we've noted, was "many." "*Increasingly it is that we all are 'many' religions. And I hope it continues.*"[27] Even the teachers of Buddhism, Sufi *dhikr* (recollection of the divine) and Hindu meditation had been heavily influenced, they told us, by one another's teachings. The Sufis have read the Buddhists and the eco-feminists, and they in turn have read the Sufis' stories and esoteric Christianity. Most in the Grassroots Spirituality Movement are tossing together their own salad of religions and beliefs out of our world-wide religious smorgasbord.

> "The books on the floor near my meditation cushions are the New Testament, an old Catholic missal, the Dao de Jing, modern Taoist meditations and currently, Jon Kabat-Zinn's *Wherever you Go, There You Are*. The latter keeps me in touch with the Buddha statue on a low rattan table with lit candle, joined by a Russian icon of Mary, who doesn't seem to mind the company; looking down on all this is a portrait of Gerard Manley Hopkins."[28]

The shibboleth-shattering point is this: unless you live in a closed or censoring community like the Amish, Hasids (which officially ban TV and radio) or some other fundamentalist group, it is now virtually impossible to believe that any one religious tradition holds the *only* truth. Functionally we are all henotheists, that is, believers in our own God as ultimate without denying the ultimacy of other Gods.[29]

This is a huge shift! A few centuries ago, everyone in a town or community would agree that "of course Jesus is God," or "of course one should not eat meat with milk." Unquestioned assumptions about the universe were an unspoken part of a shared community life. One could count on neighbors, classmates and workmates to share, in large part, one's presuppositions and daily rhythms. Even if there were disagreements, people assumed that they knew the generally "right" way to do things and the general outlines of the "true" nature of reality. But by now it is eminently clear that others may not share our views. In our pluralistic context, no belief carries the old feeling of inevitability. All truths now seem in part self-constructed, concoctions in a pluralistic world.

> *"In today's world there is an incredible diversity of belief. The clashes in values are much more 'in your face' than in earlier times. And facing that uncertainty, we desire certainty."*[30]

For religions of fixed beliefs and unchanging rituals especially, this problem of pluralism is immense.

On the other hand, Grassroots Spirituality, as we have seen, has left its theology and worldview pretty vague. It emphasizes the non-verbal and not-strictly-rational. It suggests that spirituality has to do with the intuitive and that which is "beyond words." And it focuses on ineffable experiences of the infinite. Such loosely defined spirituality offers the *experience* of a religious ultimate, while remaining verbally hazy enough to embrace a variety of (potentially contradictory) beliefs. For example, when Sufi leader Suhrawardi Gebel defined his ultimate as "*Allah, the Hindu Brahman, Buddhist Emptiness, Christ Consciousness or whatever else one might call it*," he was articulating something which was, logically speaking, profoundly inconsistent. Yet he did not feel obliged to deal with those potential dissonances. Such spiritual flexibility and openness, it should be clear, is a perfect response to the "context" of the pluralistic smorgasbord.

In such a pluralistic context, people are picking and choosing, and doing so on the basis of their own experiential evidence. We all share a relatively unconscious experimental attitude: roughly "if this works for me, or is able to solve my life problems, then I'll adopt it. Otherwise, I'll try something else." Many people told us that they had tried Buddhist meditation or TM, then went on to experiment with Sufism or Shamanism until something clicked for them. Shaman leader Michael Harner mentioned that many participants come to one or two shamanism seminars, and do not follow up.[31] This indicates, he believes, a healthy experimental attitude.

In this willingness to spiritually experiment, we may be witnessing an unanticipated consequence of our scientific attitude: spirituality is now chosen on the basis of relatively short-term personal experimentation. This may tend, however, towards a market-driven spirituality, which may be leading us towards superficiality. Arthur Zajonc may be right:

> "*perhaps there is an inflation of the smorgasbord effect. Perhaps we all have the same, unthoughtful, bland cuisine on our plates.*"[32]

This may be looked at in another way though. Moving from one practice to another may also represent an increasing discrimination in the best sense of the word. People may be dissatisfied for good reason, and moving on may be towards greater and more effective possibilities.

The Loss of Faith in Science and Rationality

This quasi-scientific, experimental attitude is ironic, given that many feel that one reason that spirituality has grown is that the scientific, rational paradigm has "let us down."

Over and over people told us this. Over the past four hundred years we have grown to believe that science and rationality would be able to solve all of our problems. It has given us so much: medicine, longer life, space exploration, televisions, and microwaves, physics, atomic fusion, and the big bang. Science was IT, we thought. It was only a matter of time before those fellows in the white coats would figure it all out. Part of the modern worldview was an arrogant but possibly naive faith in the power of human reason and the experimental attitude.

For a combination of reasons, however, we have come to think that maybe science and linear thinking alone do not work as well as we had believed. "We are slowly. . . beginning to understand that the rational consciousness . . . is an evolutionary cul-de-sac, that our monochrome vision is at the root of many of today's countless social, economic, political and ecological problems."[33] There are lots of causes for this disillusionment:

- Most overtly, some of the horrors and oversights of modern science have given us pause: the creation of the Atomic bomb, the holocaust, thalidomide babies, environmental disasters, pollution, the spread of "weapons of mass destruction, " etc. Science and technology have made some enormous, and costly, mistakes. And, but for a few notable exceptions, the scientists themselves hadn't warned us. Indeed, despite the all-knowing air, they probably hadn't seen them coming.

  "We see the miracles science has wrought and we also see what damage it has enabled us to create. Great strides in information and communication, technologies, transportation and health care have come packaged with great environmental destruction and the near loss of indigenous lifestyles around the world."[34]

- Scientists now seem to be working for the highest bidder, no matter what the effects. The men and women in the white coats have been seen to be making more addictive cigarettes, inventing more profitable and expensive drugs, polluting more rivers, developing even more devastating weapons and selling them to unscrupulous "arms merchants."

- There is a deeper frustration with science. People are questioning its atomism, its tendency to divide things up in order to understand them. We break up the atom, we slice up DNA to understand diseases, and we dissect the brain to understand human consciousness. But this divide-and-conquer attitude seems to miss something essential: ecological connections, consciousness itself, and the subtle whatever-it-is that we call "life," etc.

> *"The modern focus on objectivity and the separation of science and spirituality, taken to fullness, leaves people separate from one another, separate from nature, and separate from the divine. . . . Life in these times calls for an end to science as the primary means of influence and an opening of the pathways of influence to diverse ways of knowing."*[35]

- Though most are grateful for electricity, phones, airplanes and automobiles, fax machines and computers, many of our respondents sense that technology has also caused great damage. Much of our busyness, late nights and speed- induced anxieties may be attributed to society's technologically enhanced conveniences like light bulbs, TVs, stereos and walkmans. Technology itself is a mixed blessing.

- But by far the most insidious disappointment is that science and rationality just cannot provide meaning, value or the sense of fulfillment. Logic alone just cannot provide us with the sense that life is meaningful.

> *"Science,"* said one dissatisfied scientist, *"develops principles and then generalizes them about the world. But it diminishes the whole question of value. In doing so it misses what's important. What makes life valuable is not the orderly systemic character of life, but the idiosyncratic aspects of someone's life. Humans just are idiosyncratic, and that is what makes life interesting."* [36]

"The scientific worldview was of a universe composed entirely of objective processes, all described not in I-language or we-language, but merely in it-language, with no consciousness, no interiors, no values, no meaning, no depth and no Divinity."[37]

In short, many educated people are increasingly suspicious of science and rationality. And, we might point out, it is this very group, the highly educated urban middle class, that has been the cauldron out of which Grassroots Spirituality has emerged.

Disillusionment with the American Dream

This frustration with science and rationality relates to another commonly noted cause of Grassroots Spirituality. Many of us are disillusioned with what many societies call the "dream of success." In America it's called the "American Dream."

"We believed that if we got the job, had a family and sent our kids to a decent school, then we'd be happy. But it was a lie."[38]

People feel that

"I'm doing everything right. I've got a job, a car, a nice house. Yet I still feel there is something wrong. There is a hole in us. We try to fill it through our craving for material things, or it leads us into drugs and alcohol. But these things don't work. Its only when we learn to fill ourselves in new more permanent ways, through the spiritual life, that we can truly fill that hole."[39]

The American Dream concealed an unstated contract: if you do these things, play the game well, pass all the tests, then you will be happy. This contract was implied by the all those advertisements: if you buy a new Ford, a new coat or a bracelet of gold, you will be happy. In all those

Horatio Algers stories, once they had become wealthy, all those poor boys and girls lived happily ever after. Those people in their minks and big houses on the hill were all supposed to be so happy. If we made money, had our white picket fences, 2.2 children, and the dog, then, finally, we would be truly fulfilled.

> *"But lo and behold we bought the dream and followed the program, and when we got to the middle of our lives we said, 'well damn, I'm just not happy. There's gotta be more than this.'"*[40]

Widely admired Ram Dass said that he had all the things that one is supposed to want: love, family, children, job, income and success. But still he was desperately unhappy.

Though it may not mean riches or fame, spirituality is seen to offer a new, richer and more deeply satisfying life. Its sense of meaning, peace, and spiritual connection promises a richer, more fulfilled life. If the heartwarming and satisfied tone of our respondents is any indicator, it may be delivering on that promise.

Historical Causes, Perennial Causes

Two last suggestions about the causes of Grassroots Spirituality have to do with the reasons about why, in general, new spiritual or religious movements develop.

There are two basic approaches to the question, which we might call historicist and essentialist. Those with an intellectual historian's mindset tend to point to the multiple threads of history that may have led to this development. The "essentialist approach" suggests that human beings may have an innate tendency towards spirituality, and our Grassroots version is just its latest manifestation.[41]

Historians that we heard from pointed to a wide range of intellectual forces that may have led to the Grassroots Spirituality Movement. Generally their "causes" varied depending on their specialty. Scholars of Christianity, for example, pointed to the development of individually oriented spiritual attitudes within the Christian churches, especially in the nineteenth and twentieth centuries. "Spirituality," they rightly say, is a Christian term, and many of its basic themes were developed there.[42] Robert Ellwood points to the general open mindedness of recent Protestantism, which encouraged its constituents to explore a variety of spiritualities.[43] Anne Taves, scholar of late Protestantism, points to the findings of William James in *The Variety of Religious Experience* as a key element in making mysticism credible. She traces a line from James to the founder of AA, Bill W., who was a Christian who probably read James. Bill W. seems to have helped make the distinction between "religion" and "spirituality" popular. Catherine Albanese, scholar of late nineteenth century religion, points out that "metaphysical" thinkers played an important role as well.[44] Scholars of Judaism rightly point to the works of Buber, Heschel and the Kabala tradition as critical, and note the growth of interest in spiritual forms of Judaism.[45]

Scholars of Buddhism point out that Buddhism was imported into the West, starting in the nineteenth century and rising to a crescendo in the middle twentieth. This importation was one of the critical factors in spirituality's growth, they claim.[46] Hinduism scholars point to Vivekenanda's famously successful appearance at the Parliament of the World's Religions in 1893 as an important formative moment in modern spirituality.

All of these insights are right, of course. None is complete.

The essentialist (or perennialist) position takes a somewhat different tack. Scholars like Huston Smith, Ken Wilber, Fritjof Schuon, Coomerswami and Aldous Huxley argue that no era has gone for long without some religious or spiritual expressions. Even in epochs like the post-Vedic (India), post- Shang-ti (China), or pre-Muslim

Bedouin (Arab) society, in which old religious systems
became outmoded and unsatisfying, it was typically less
than two centuries before some new form of religiosity
bubbled up. Human beings have always developed some
suitable religious or spiritual forms.

Why is this? There may be an innate human drive for
spirituality, or at least some form of religiosity. One might
take a Darwinian view of this, and suggest that spirituality
emerges as a way to keep people sane or comfortable
under life's trying circumstances — a kind of survival tool.
Or spirituality may emerge, as Herbert Benson suggests,
as a way for the human nervous system to regain a balance
and regenerate itself. We humans, in this view, may be
hard-wired for spirituality.

Whatever the reason, our species has shown a remarkably steady tendency to perceive a religious or spiritual
reality over its many centuries. As other forms of religiosity have fallen by the wayside over the past century, we
may be witnessing the development of a new set of spiritual claims, which are more appropriate for our day and
worldview. In sum, Grassroots Spirituality may just be
our incarnation of a fundamental drive.

This weighty debate between the essentialists and the
historians is of a piece with the 2500 year old debate
between the followers of Plato and Aristotle. And it is well
beyond my modest abilities to resolve.

But I can predict that if the Grassroots Spirituality
Movement is generally recognized to exist, there will be a
great rush of credit-taking by traditions, historians, theoreticians and traditional defenders, all claiming to be the
"real" source of its birth and development. The Hindu,
Christian, Jewish, and transcendentalist scholars will all
point to their piece of the pie and argue that *this* is what
really caused this phenomenon.

And of course, they will all be right! Vivekananda,
Christian developments, Buber, Buddhist teachers, and so
on all did play their important roles.

But these scholars and tradition defenders will all be incomplete too. There are indeed threads and strands within each of them that have led our civilization in this important new direction. All these various streams have fed this new river.

But no one of these thinkers can tell us just why their preferred sources began to all point in just *this* particular direction just when they did. For that we need other answers as well.

The essentialists may be right too; there does seem to be some natural human tendency to be spiritual. We may indeed be a Homo Spiritus. But this explanation does not help us understand just why spirituality emerged *in just this way* in the late twentieth century? Again, we need the other reasons too.

In other words, all of these are necessary pieces of the puzzle. But none of them alone is the whole answer. Alone, none of these threads or social forces or belief shifts created this enormous movement. That's the nature of something that is *overdetermined*.

Conclusions

Like any huge social movement, Grassroots Spirituality is overdetermined. It has many various, loosely intersecting yet redundant causes, any one of which could have potentially caused it. It is a response to a wide, interconnected and redundant set of demographic shifts, historical factors, human forces and social evolutions. It answers to the human longings that have resulted from a shift from relatively static and tradition-orientated rural settings to today's fast-changing cities and technological developments. It addresses the pain and chafing we unconsciously feel about the loss of coherent family structures and steady communities. It is filling the holes in our hearts left as the churches and synagogues could no longer maintain the illusion that they had the "sole truth." It is a response to the loss of faith in science, technology and rationality that we feel, as well as our disappointment with the dream of success. It provides us with a sense of deeper meaning in our lives that our highly controlled lives have left out. It offers new, more solid sets of values and life-goals than did mere materialism. It is the expression of many intersecting historical forces. And it is our expression of a fundamental human urge to discover and experience the spiritual reality.

With such a confluence of forces, it is hardly surprising that Grassroots Spirituality has emerged with such force.

Notes — Chapter VII

[1] Anne and Charles Simpkinson, "Feeding One Another," *Common Boundary*, vol. 16, (no. 6) November 1998, p. 22.
[2] Mary Pipher, *The Shelter of Each Other: Rebuilding our Families*. Quoted in Ibid.
[3] Robert Wuthnow, p. 5.
[4] Jeffry Steven Gaines, Executive Director, Spiritual Directors International.
[5] RKC
[6] Robert Wuthnow, p.47.
[7] Eugene Taylor, "Desperately Seeking Spirit," *Psychology Today*, November, 1994, pp. 56–68.
[8] Wade Clark Roof, *A Generation of Seekers* (San Francisco, 1994), p. 122 ff.
[9] KD
[10] RKC
[11] KD
[12] J. Gordon Melton, "Another Look at New Religions," in *Religion: North American Style*, ed. Thomas Dowdy and Patrick McNamara (New Brunswick, NJ: Rutgers University Press, 1997), p. 185.
[13] SE
[14] Ken Suibielski
[15] Stuart Smithers, reporting on a study done about the growing interest in Buddhism and other eastern religions commissioned by the Catholic church.
[16] Lonnie Kleiver. Considering the enormous numbers of active Christians, and the influence of the church as a whole, this is probably an oversimplification.
[17] RKC
[18] SJ
[19] Robin Norcross
[20] Jack Healey
[21] Paul Ray, The Cultural Creatives.
[22] Martin Rutte
[23] See here Robert K. C. Forman, *Meister Eckhart: Mystic as Theologian* (London: Element Books, 1991).
[24] Nancy Ammerman
[25] As pointed out by J. Gordon Melton.
[26] Martin Rutte
[27] Paul Walsh
[28] Eugene Bianchi, "Trans Traditional Spirituality" *Corpus Reports*, September–October 1997, p. 7.

[29] This term, coined in the nineteenth century by Max
       Mueller, signifies the belief in one god as ultimate without
       denying the ultimacy of other gods. Of course, Mueller
       applied this to the Vedic system. I am applying it to today's
       multi-religious pluralistic situation, in which we each hold
       that our gods and religions express the ultimate, but at the
       same time we do not deny that another's system or God
       may also be ultimate.
[30] Lynn Huber
[31] MH
[32] Arthur Zajonc
[33] Georg Feuerstein, quoted by Barbara Schultz.
[34] Diana Whitney, "Spirituality as an Organizing Principle,"
       World Business Academy Perspectives, vol. 9, no. 4, 1995, p.
       51.
[35] Ibid, p. 61.
[36] KD
[37] Ken Wilber, *The Marriage of Sense and Soul* (NY: Random
       House, 1998), p. 56.
[38] SJ
[39] Sharif Abdullah
[40] KD
[41] Lynn Huber
[42] Anne Taves suggested this at the Santa Barbara consulta-
       tion on spirituality, March, 1998.
[43] Robert Ellwood suggested this at the Santa Barbara consul-
       tation on spirituality, March, 1998.
[44] Cathrine Albinese suggested this at the Santa Barbara con-
       sultation on spirituality, March, 1998.
[45] Tamar Frankiel pointed here at the same conference.
       Arthur Waskow suggested this as well.
[46] Stuart Smithers

Chapter VIII

Institutional Inroads

*We need to ask the question how does a whole
society become more spiritually open? . . . Now
some work too much and others not enough.
What ought to be the relationship between work
and rest? How can every person have access
to decent work and also to a decent amount of
rest.*[1]

Arthur Waskow

In attempting to learn how spirituality is or is not being
brought into society's institutions, we focused our
interviews and researches on spirituality in two institutions, the workplaces of business and government, and the
medical and health care systems.

In these explorations, we discovered several patterns.
First, whatever else may be said, as a civilization we are
very early in the process of bringing spirituality into our
workplaces and institutions. The bad news is it has *only*
begun: the numbers of people doing this work is small, the
percent of offices and hospitals that are exploring how to
integrate spirituality is still tiny, and the procedures are
but seminal. But the good news is, it has *clearly* begun.

Weaving spirituality into our workplace is not a new
idea. In most other ages and lands, spirituality or religion
was understood to be profoundly integrated with everything people did: work, social relationships, community
celebrations, medicine, etc. For example, India's farming

techniques, marriage rules and governmental structures were all highly shaped by its deities and its religiously based caste system. Choice of marriage mate, dietary and cleanliness patterns, celebrations — all were profoundly integrated with the religious system. Similarly Muslim work patterns, marriage structures and government laws were guided by the Koran, the way of Mohammed as known through the Hadith literature, and the religious law, the *shari'a*. Work lives in medieval "Christendom" were understood to be seamlessly connected with the priesthood, the papacy, and with God Himself. After the Reformation, work lives and institutional structures remained religiously shaped under the notion of "*cujus regio ejus religio*," the religion of the prince shall be the religion of the state.[2] The institutions of the church and the state were inextricably linked. Lutheranism, Calvinism and other main Protestant denominations saw all work as the expression of a divine task. Similarly Jews throughout the Common Era have kept the Sabbath, worked under Talmudic law, and eaten according to the laws of Kosher.

But as in so much else, America and the modern Western world is different. For the first time in history, a nation was founded with a constitutional declaration that no one, not even the state, can *insist* that another must believe or worship in any particular way. Such separation has clearly become the *de facto*, if not the *de jure*, law of virtually every other modernized or westernized society. While this rule is imperfectly enforced and obeyed, it clearly has set the problematic for modern American institutional life.

For it leaves us with the difficult question of how can a government or an institution integrate spirituality into its broader structures yet not *impose* any particular dogma or beliefs onto its employees, constituents, etc. How can a corporation or non-profit integrate some spiritual or religious principles into its statement of purpose or charter yet allow a member to disagree, refuse or even challenge that institutions' religio- spiritual principles? How can we create more spiritually fulfilling institutions without crossing the first amendment's principle of the freedom of religion?

Yet despite the difficulties, our civilization — America and the other industrialized nations — is now struggling to integrate open and non-dogmatic spiritual principles into our institutions. Despite the strides we have made, we have barely begun.

Spirituality in the Workplace

We observed previously that there is a great deal of disillusionment about the dream of success. People are feeling that even though they worked hard, played by the rules and earned a good living, they are not feeling satisfied. Both bored line-workers and their managers struggle with this, the dissatisfaction of the successful. Even well-to-do business leaders we spoke with are feeling the need for more depth and meaning in their lives. Indeed many are leading the re-spiritualization of the workplace.

Many of them have recognized that there are good business reasons for changing the way we work. Business consultant Christopher Schaefer, who writes on business and spirituality, wrote:

> "In 1994 a national commission on productivity estimated that half of the work force expends only the minimal energy needed to get by, and that only two of ten employees work at close to full potential. In many large organizations feelings of alienation, isolation and powerlessness are widespread, leading to high levels of absenteeism and to stress, anxiety and depression. Spiritual and contemplative disciplines . . . can contribute significantly to helping organizations gain a clear and shared sense of mission, a sense of community between people, and an

individual and organization's commitment to learning."³

A disillusioned and demoralized workforce cannot work
up to its potential. This is known to be especially important to the more creative teams, each corporation's "Skunk
Works," whose job it is to invent the products, develop the
lines, or rewrite the rules. Not surprisingly, it is these corporate creatives who, along with personnel departments,
are among the leaders in bringing spirituality into the
institutions.

> *"Those who report utilizing various intentional and con-
> templative disciplines at work say that their effective-
> ness, concentration and ability to handle whatever arises
> are clearly enhanced."*⁴

Another factor, which sociologists call "the time bind,"
is driving spirituality into the workplace. The boundaries
between families and work have shifted. Parents are very
busy these days, with both parents often working long
hours. Their children are often either with some nanny for
many hours or are latch-key children. Such children can
be very demanding when the parents finally do come
home. Thus the old fount of spirituality, the family hearth,
is now often a place of harried moments, hardly conducive
to quiet or self- reflection. Churches too have lost their
attraction as safe havens for many, for reasons outlined in
Chapter VII.

Thus ironically enough, spirituality may develop more
easily within the workplace than in the traditional family
or church settings. Working places and corporations may
be rising to meet these more personal and spiritual needs.
Many corporations and hospitals now offer day care centers, psychological counseling centers, and even structure
processes that foster people's personal and spiritual
growth.

Horses for Courses

Though again we are early in this process of spiritualizing our workplaces, it has very definitely begun:

> *"Spirituality is already quite widespread in our institutions. It's in all aspects of business. There are many organizations involved. In some organizations it's more up front, but there are many people who are seeking more meaning in their lives."*[5]

Primarily, the business managers and consultants involved in this process are encouraging the growth of spirit in two general directions: organizationally and personally. Though a few, like the Shalem Institute, do use the "S-word," most do not talk in traditional "spiritual" terms, but rather are tailoring their language to "fit" the corporate mindset.

A recent spiritual leader in the World Bank told us,

> *"It is good to tailor the language to those people to whom you are talking. You will lose people if you miss their level. With some people you can converse about spirituality, reincarnation, astrology, channeling or even extra terrestrials. But to others you can't. Similarly, it's good to tailor the teaching for each group. We have an expression in England, 'Horses for courses.' (That is, certain horses run better on certain courses.) You have to couch your message in appropriate terms for the audience. We made progress at the World Bank because we used the unobjectionable word 'values.'"*[6]

> *"In our consulting work we talk about the process of overcoming bias or blind spots or counterproductive assumptions, not 'spirituality.'"*[7]

> *"[We speak of] putting workplace spirit into the context of economic results and long term strategic viability."*[8]

> *"In business I don't often use the word spirituality. I meet people where they are and then move with them.*

*Thus I talk about dialogue, getting our cards on the table,
and so on. I try to be practical with them."*[9]

Recognizing that the bottom line is still key, consultants
who are bringing spirituality to businesses — primarily
organizational development consultants and personnel
managers — are talking of spirituality in the language of
corporations:

> *"increasing efficiency when employees are satisfied"* and
> *"integrity, values, visions, openness to diversity, and
> high employee moral. [We're talking] about fostering
> relationships and creating an environment that fosters
> each person's creativity,"*[10]

and

> *"a corporate value statement that evolves and
> changes."*[11]

After all, religious sounding language is loaded with
baggage. It seems to many to be a code word for "dogma,"
and it smacks of enforced belief and imposed behavioral
rules. According to management consultant Martin Rutte,
many managers and workers fear having some old religious dogmatism shoved down their throats. Recognizing
this, Rutte makes it a point to not present spirituality as *the*
answer.

> *"When spirituality is presented as an answer it becomes
> dogma. That doesn't allow people to do their own search-
> ing."*[12]

Instead he presents spirituality as an attitude of ongoing
questioning,

> *"allowing the door to be opened if you choose. Thus our
> job is to make spiritual inquiry safe and permissible, and
> to have conversations about spirituality in the workplace,
> if people choose."*[13]

Leaders of the (Business) Pack

Spirituality is being championed in the business and institutional communities by a mix of advocates. Leading the way are the Organizational Development (OD) consultants. Jim Berry estimates that roughly a third of the attendees at a typical spirituality in business conferences he produces are OD consultants, trainers and consulting facilitators.

A second group is employees of large corporations, typically personnel managers and people who are responsible for corporate ethics. It is they who recognize most clearly that in an era of downsizing people can no longer count on IBM or Citibank for security, even if they've worked there all their lives. This can be threatening to morale, for even those who are still employed are being asked to work harder to make up for those let go.

"There is an old unwritten agreement: if I give my life's work to you, the corporation, then you will take care of me. But in the era of downsizing this logic is now gone. People are feeling insecure."[14]

Spirituality, many personnel managers feel, is one answer to this morale problem. These leaders are seeking ways to help their employees find, even within the corporate cubicle, deeper and more spiritual values.

A third group leading the spirituality wave are the heads of the creativity sections, a corporation's "Skunk Works." As mentioned above, these are the inventors, designers and others whose job it is to stay ahead of their field. They know that creativity is not a strictly linear, logical process, and that often the more intuitive "hunches" are the most creative. When people are feeling worried or protective of their jobs or their turf, they are not at their most creative. Spiritual processes, in which one sounds the intuitive depths, are often seen as helpful.

*"Companies are dependent on creativity. These groups
tend to be organizationally loose. Many in fast moving
industries… feel that they have to be spiritual to stay
ahead."*[15]

Surprisingly, however, one of the largest groups that is
leading the spiritual wave in business, if The Message
Company's attendees are any measure, are the managers,
CEOs and other leaders of corporate management.[16] Their
corporations' success is their main concern, and these people are exploring whether and how spirituality and an
increasing attention to depth may help.

The fourth major group that is bringing spirituality to
business is the leadership of small corporations. Here the
story is more serendipitous. If a small corporation has an
owner or manager who is particularly sympathetic to
deeper values, he or she can tell employees that "dialogue
is something I think will be good for the company" and
they will be likely to experiment with it. Many small (250
employees or less) companies are particularly open to
exploring these issues. Matters tend to become more complicated in a publicly traded corporations, in which management has to answer to thousands of stockholders.
Weaving subtler values into their corporate life becomes a
more complex, though clearly not impossible, task.

* * *

Spirituality in Medicine
by Kathryn Davison

Every culture's approach to the nature and treatment of
illness is shaped by its spiritual theories, formal or informal. In ancient times, for instance, mental illness was
regarded as a sign of demonic possession; so patients'
skulls were pierced or drilled to let the evil spirits out. In a
famous biblical healing encounter, Jesus was asked by his
disciples, "What has this man done, or has his father done,

that he is rendered blind?" Such a question presupposes the belief that suffering is a form of punishment for one's sins or the sins of one's father. Over the centuries healing and spirituality were generally believed to go hand in hand. This link was dropped by modern medicine. Healing became divorced from one's deeper spiritual life. Yet over the last 25 years, the connection between spirituality and healing has been again emerging.

The push for bringing spirituality into the health care world has come up from three interrelated directions, and we have organized this section around them:

1. **The Patient**. A health crisis often precipitates a spiritual crisis. If my life is to be shortened or compromised, how can I best cope with it? What is the likelihood of an afterlife? What aspects of life make it worth enduring the struggle in the face of suffering? Is the nature of one's health problem symbolic, a meaningful sign of the issues that brought it about? What kind of God lets babies die?

2. **Doctors and Nurses**. Some doctors and nurses have recently been weaving spiritual values into the health care system. Obviously, the compassion they demonstrate as they work to alleviate suffering is inherently spiritual. The binding of wounds, the gentleness of care, the healing relationship between the professional and the patient — all of these comprise medicine's spiritual fabric. But recently spirituality's connection to healing is being explored anew. Increasing attention is being directed towards the value of a spiritual life and the effect of prayer on healing. Meditation has sometimes been used as part and parcel of healthcare. Researchers are exploring how spiritual beliefs might promote good health. Once strictly rationalistic and reductionistic health care agents are beginning to ask how and when to integrate spiritual processes into

contemporary medical practice. Should doctors and nurses also be shamans? If so, how?

3. **Medical theoreticians**. Some thinkers are reconsidering the assumptions of medicine. They are asking, how does spirit meet matter? How might their relationship effect healing? What is "spontaneous remission" and what might help it? Might spiritual healers do what they claim? Does spirituality work only within the patient's brain, or does it tap a power from within and beyond the individual?[17] Science and spirituality have traditionally been strange bedfellows, but some of the most progressive minds are now exploring their juncture in ways that may point to a fundamental restructuring of our world views.

These are the themes that emerged in the comments of the individuals we interviewed about spirituality in health care.

The Patient

For many individuals, life is a series of events to be marked and managed like an errand list . . . until a health crisis comes along. "I'm sorry to have to tell you. Your biopsy results are positive." One's entire sense of normalcy collapses to an abrupt halt. All the errands of the day, all the routines and weekend plans dissolve in waves of fear, shock, and chaos. One finds oneself pondering, often for the first time, existential issues. All of a sudden, life seems deeply impermanent, tenuous. One often clings to the everyday in an entirely new way. One woman, who had a heart attack at 47, said,

> *"I continue to think that one day or the next will be my last day. I weep because I haven't danced at my daughter's wedding . . . and I cling to this life with all of the intensity I can muster."*

For many, the illness itself comes to seem deeply meaningful. It becomes a sign that one is not living one's life in accordance with an authentically spiritual direction. This kind of reaction implicitly presupposes that there is a right way and a wrong way to live, and that knowledge of the "right way" is implicitly spiritual. Their disease, then, becomes a sign of spiritual disconnection and an opportunity to reconnect:

> *"Well, there was a twenty-four month period when we buried seven family members, inherited a business (out of town) and commuted back and forth between here and Dallas to take the children to school. My son was having academic problems, my daughter developed anorexia, and I developed thyroid cancer. There were so many wakeup calls, in fact. Maybe I'm a slow learner."*[18]

Freud,[19] Alexander,[20] and a host of others have speculated that psychological factors, often unconscious, underlay many of their clients' "somatic" health symptoms. Disease, in this psychosomatic model, constitutes a meaningful, non-verbal cue. But few patients actually report that their illness carries psychological import or think that something like unresolved anger toward their mother produces their back pain. Rather, they often see it as a spiritual omen, a sign that takes them out of their mundane mindset and shifts their attention to ultimate values.

It is natural then that many patients turn to a spiritual practice as an important coping method. Because of their suffering, it all of a sudden seems a natural time to pray, to get in touch with a higher power, or to acknowledge that one's ultimate fate is outside of one's own power.

> *"I gave it all to God. I am not a religious person, but in doing this, in giving it to God, in knowing that he knows my fears − that he loves me so much that he gave me this life and all the attributes of living here at this time − that*

surely he will see me through this transfer of life — and in that I have faith."

Somehow, for those whose lives are at critical turning points, one's sensed relationship with the ultimate seems to become salient, necessary and nearly palpable. There is comfort, many told us, in giving up the sense of control.

Doctors and Nurses

To find out about the status of spirituality in mainstream health care, we focused our interviews not on a-traditional healers but on more traditional ("allopathic") doctors and nurses. And some health care providers have indeed begun to weave spirituality into their practices. In our interviews with them, we heard this refrain:

"People are hungry for what science doesn't do. They want care, a healing touch, not just your intellectual input." [21]

Another said,

"If these people are helped to ask the right questions, if someone listens and is present to them through their difficult time, it's transformative, and they remember it forever. . . You've got to have people in medicine who understand the value of that relational component, who understand it experientially, not academically." [22]

Our spiritually-minded health care practitioners generally held that medicine has focused on addressing symptoms and on some means of *curing* through artificial techniques (drugs, surgery, etc.) to the exclusion of the personal side of *healing*. The relational aspect that is often so highly valued by patients is often regarded as soft headed by doctors, an also-ran in the treatment agenda that detracts from their precise one-pointed focus on disease and prescription. But our interviewees felt that patients who are only treated medically are being robbed of the essential value of their suffering: its meaning. Only love and compassion can help make that visible. One surgical-room healing agent quipped, "*You know, the idea of loving your patients passionately is not exactly 'au courant' in medicine.*"[23]

This lack is, according to the more spiritually-minded health care providers, a mistake, and the remnant of either/or thinking. "*Medicine is a servant science,*" says Ron Anderson, "*You may be privileged due to your high level of expertise (as an MD), but you are also privileged because the patient respects you. So you have a higher responsibility, a duty to know and honor the patient.*"[24] Doctors, nurses, and chaplains who see that a health crisis is also a spiritual crisis know that the healing process only occurs if the whole person is heard, understood, and helped. As one hospital chaplain illustrated:

> "*Let's say that there's a fetus condition that is incompatible with life. The people on the (treatment) team need to say this is hard, this is a hard choice this family is making out of love. . . Pastoral care is about saying, 'I've been here before and this is new and scary for you, but other people have walked this part of the path and lived to tell about it.' The point is these are issues that cannot be decided through logic, but through the choices made with the heart.*"[25]

Recently, however, spirituality has begun to find its way into mainstream medicine. One recent pioneer is Herbert Benson. Intrigued by the implications from the well known placebo effect, Benson and his colleagues cast about for a way to harness a meaningful placebo that would enhance recovery prospects in various patient groups. Religion was a natural fit. "*Basically, the most powerful belief in America is the religious belief. It forms a basis for healing that way.*"[26] Benson asserts that prayerful practice may be a powerful aspect of self-care often left out of the health care equation. His carefully controlled studies indi-

cate that those who engage in the assigned spiritual practices experienced significant physiological, psychological,
and health benefits. Dubbed the "relaxation response," he
found that meditative and prayer practices reduced cate-
cholamines (neurotransmitters indicative of stress and
arousal), heart rates, blood pressure, and brought about
other changes associated with reduced stress.

Benson's work and others' has built a vital bridge
between the patients' sense of the importance of belief and
meaning, and the health care professionals. Humans may
be, suggests Benson, *"hard wired for God."*[27] The body and
the psyche both respond to that sense of loving, sustaining
presence that is the hallmark of spiritual feeling. And
those who organize their life around spiritual values seem
on average to have greater well-being, higher social integration, and, yes, better health.

Spiritual practices have become central features of an
important handful of mind–body health clinics. Figures
such as Jon Kabat-Zinn, Joan Borysenko, Dean Ornish and
James Gordon are attempting to demonstrate the value of
spiritual practices for health care. Hypertensives, chronic
pain patients, and heart attack sufferers are gathering at
their centers across the US to meditate together and are
participating in small groups. Studies suggest that they
are reducing the severity of their respective health
challenges.

Many if not most of these programs, we note, draw
heavily on a support group or group-process model.

In sum, our interviewees consistently claimed that
when the patients' spiritual issues (meaning, values, and
connection) are included in their treatment program, they
are more likely to be cured or better adapted to their illness. When stress and anxiety are reduced, and meaning is
increased, healing is more likely to happen.

Outside the clinic or hospital setting, spiritual small
groups have been effectively harnessed for other forms of
health care. It would be hard to overstate the importance

of the AA movement, for example, in healing the lives of millions of alcoholics. Of the famed "twelve steps" outlined by "Bill W" in the 1920s, the *first* step is to acknowledge that only a higher power could empower the individual to overcome the urge to drink. He also recommended making amends for the damage done under its influence to friends, coworkers, and family members — another spiritual principle. It is striking that the single largest means of health behavior change in the United States is effected through this free, anonymous, loosely organized network of spiritually oriented support groups. The twelve-step model has now been successfully extended to address a number of other health challenges: obesity, anorexia, drug addiction and even to children of alcoholics. On the internet and in churches, colleges, hospitals and even in shopping malls, patients are gathering in small groups to support each other through their experiences of addiction withdrawal, illness, and recovery, and to try to come to terms with their meaning.

Another rapidly growing area of health care, we heard, is alternative medicine. The more spiritual holistic orientation evident in these programs may represent a meeting ground between patient and professional. Strict biomedicine seems to be waning, giving way to a number of other health care approaches, as indicated by the results of a large study recently conducted by Eisenberg.[28] To everyone's surprise, more visits were made to alternative medicine practitioners in a single year than were made to primary care physicians: what was once considered a fringe alternative is now recognized as an international shift in health care choice. The factor that distinguishes practitioners of alternative medicine from their more traditional counterparts is their worldview: alternative paradigms consider the health problem as part and parcel of the patient's whole life. This is clearly of a piece with Grassroots Spirituality, in which growth and personal insight are engendered through a broader understanding of health and illness.

Theoreticians of Medicine

These trends in self-help and in holistic care-seeking suggest a fundamental shift in the underlying *orientation* of health care. A great debate has begun about the nature of the body and of healing. At some point, we may have to decide whether health problems are the product of bad genes and environmental exposure, or if they stem from more transcendent causes, reflecting some imperfect match of a soul's purpose and a body's conduct. Modern medicine, as currently practiced, is a technologically advanced but narrow focus on disease processes and the arrest of those processes. Within such a model, death is a failure and cure is the only goal. Those who assert a spiritual approach view disease as part of a larger journey. Thus their highest goal is the unleashing of our capacity to experience a richer life: human and social values such as love, truth, peace, creativity and compassion are taken as indexes of health.

To many in medicine, it is evident that spiritual practice itself can have both a curative and restorative value. But many doctors feel uncomfortable with the whole idea of a spiritual dimension, because such a worldview presumes the existence of causal factors that cannot be viewed under a microscope.

Furthermore to accept the spiritual approach would open a Pandora 's Box of possibilities: is it possible for prayers to effect healing at a distance? Is there life after death? Are miracles wrought through some special cooperation with the divine? Medicine is facing a metaphysical identity crisis, and the debate is unsettling for a number of reasons.

For one thing, it poses several catch-22s for the more spiritually oriented scientists. First, their scientific work life and their personal attitudes may be experienced as in conflict. Says one mystically-inclined immunologist:

> *"There are moments when I'm walking along the beach, and I can feel the sun on my skin or something, and I am struck with a sense or an awareness of the oneness of myself in concert with nature. If I try to analyze the experience, it destroys it. Music is likewise a transformative experience for me, and although you can analyze it, nowhere in the analysis will you find what makes it transformative."*[29]

For him logic has its limits. Though he recognizes that medical treatments are supposed to be generated by strictly rational, scientific procedures, this leaves out a great deal.

> *"The goal of science is to make general assumptions. There's no room for the idiosyncratic or the individual; it doesn't matter because it detracts from those general principles."*[30]

Similarly, Larry Dossey says,

> *"The task of science is to render the world less mysterious, to define the great unknowns."*

Behind this medical debate stands another conundrum. Traditional scientists tend to divide a problem or a phenomenon into a series of constituent parts. Yet others have begun to ask if the *whole* can be explained in terms of its constituent parts. For example, does a man die of heart disease because his wife left him, because he works hard to avoid the pain of his wife leaving him, because he smokes to stay alert while he works, because he drinks in excess to relax when he gets home, because he is chronically angry and suspicious of his ex-wife and others, because he overeats, or because he inherited his tendencies from his father before him, who had a similar temperament and fate? Our poor fellow could be given

anti-drinking medicine, anti-smoking medicine, choles-
terol- lowering drugs, and anti-depressants. Would he
thereby be healed? Is it enough to research solutions to
health problems at the molecular level alone?

For academic scientists, researching spiritual solutions
to "molecular problems" is generally a career-ender.
When asked about his spiritual life in the context of work,
one biologist remarked,

> *"I was just thinking about how difficult it is for biological
> scientists to discuss spirituality in their workplace
> because they're supposed to assume it doesn't exist."*[31]

Disgusted with science as it was practiced, this researcher
quit his tenured position at a prominent medical school
and moved to the Caribbean.

> *"I could think better without the confinement of the
> industry through which you have to get grants. If you
> don't support the belief system, you don't get grants."*[32]

Thus, one obvious limitation of today's science is the
entrenched institutional position of reductionism and
economics.

Conclusions

The modern scientific paradigm is a powerful shaper of
thought and action. But the paradigm itself may be changing. Scientific and spiritual issues are converging in the
healing arts. The pressure to change comes in part from
patients who are seeking to increase the sense of meaning
in their lives, and to harness spiritual practices as a means
to recovery and relief. Data, to some extent, drives the
change: a variety of empirical observations point to a
strange and wonderful link between the physical and the
ephemeral.

These are descriptive aspects. What prescriptive steps
are suggested by these considerations? Certainly, despite

some initial discomfort, modern medicine seems to be moving to respect and embrace spirituality as an effective tool for healing. Through small groups, patients are already making important changes in health behaviors, learning valuable stress and pain management exercises, and rediscovering the value of spiritual practice. They are talking to and supporting each other, trying to understand their illnesses within their unique life stories, and encouraging each other to take the steps necessary to unfold a fuller life. In some cases, therapeutic support groups that have included a therapeutic aspect have succeeded where all other medical interventions failed. In the case of heart disease, for example, Dean Ornish drew on a group model to help patients learn how to retailor their lives, demonstrating for the first time that arterial clogging could be reversed.[33] David Spiegel, likewise, reported in a sample of metastic breast cancer patients that those who participated in group psychotherapy experienced twice the survival time of their control counterparts.[34]

Small Groups have a tremendous potential of both spiritual and medical value. But the model is new, and is well-developed at only a few institutions. We believe it would be worthwhile for both scientific and spiritual reasons to facilitate more small group dialogues for people who are facing serious or chronic illness, drawing on what is known about the impact of these and other spiritual practices on health. The debate and the development of methods for spiritualizing health care are but in their early stages, but certainly the hospitals and treatment centers that encourage such practices are likely to win the heartfelt devotion of their clients.

* * *

Spiritualizing the Institutions:
A How-To Guide

In both of the institutions we looked at, spiritual conversations, spiritual inquiry and a willingness to explore with one another seem to be among the most productive keys to bringing spirituality into our institutions. Through an ongoing and regular series of non-dogmatic, exploratory dialogues in business settings, 12-step meetings, Bible Study groups and other loosely structured conversations, people have found opportunities to identify and explore their deeper values and dreams with one another, and thus to share on a deeper spiritual level. Such dialogues allow people, advocates claim, to open up to and support each other in deep ways. Such conversations, loosely associated with our institutions, both support individuals' personal growth, and often become occasions to articulate values that may clarify the group's and the institution's shared vision, problems and possible new directions. In business they may serve not only to raise employee morale, especially under the looming clouds of downsizing, possible bankruptcies or the loss of faith in the corporate management, but may also help to clarify the corporation's long-term directions. In medicine they may both help people heal and also find meaning in their crises.

Some spiritually progressive organizations, notably non-profit corporations like *Common Boundary*, The Institute of Noetic Science, *The Open Center*, and others, have attempted to import the use of traditional spiritual tools — bells, silence, music, dance and inspirational readings — into their daily routine or their corporate meetings. The Fetzer Institute provides not only a meditation room within its impressive corporate building, but encourages its employees to take meditative "quiet time" (on company time). Such far-seeing organizations often structure institution-wide dialogues about the corporate passion and directions, and a place to air out their difficulties.

Some, notably Cris Schaefer of The High Tor Alliance, have suggested that spirituality has entered our work lives in force.[35] Our researches have not tended to confirm this assertion. Despite their success this work has reached but a tiny fraction of America's corporations and workplaces. Of those who are treading this path, most are novices. Only a small percent of for-profit corporations or even hospitals have attempted to articulate truly deeper values. Few support ongoing in-depth dialogues, and very few businesses have articulated values other than the bottom line. This movement has barely touched the Fortune 500. The top-down model still largely reigns supreme. Few mainstream doctors have organized systematic health support groups, or discuss life values with their patients. There is much work to be done here.

Yet there is reason for optimism. We believe that we are at the early stages of a huge transformation in our institutions. Spirituality in our institutions may be parallel to the PC computer industry in the early 1980s. There is healthy demand for consultants' services, but their numbers and impact are still comparatively small. It's early in the process, but there's clearly developing interest. Our institutional worlds have not yet undergone a spiritual sea-change, but this process seems to have begun. Today offers an enormous opportunity.

Conclusions: The Key is the Intimate Group

As we have seen elsewhere, one of the most effective spiritual tools in weaving spirituality into our society's institutions is the small group. Some of the biggest names in the spirituality at work field — Martin Rutte, Richard Barrett, Glenna Gerard, Angeles Arrien, and others — do their work primarily through small groups. In medicine, as we noted, along with the role of hospital chaplains the most important spiritual tool is the small support group.

Many are capitalizing on David Bohm's Dialogue Process, getting people from a variety of stripes and roles to express themselves to one another and explore their own assumptions. Says dialogue leader Glenna Gerard, *"I try to create a dialogue environment in which people feel free to express themselves and tell the truth."*[36] At my job, says another spiritually minded business person, *"we're trying to create a place where people can talk, where they are allowed to develop themselves."*[37] At the World Bank, small groups reportedly had an enormous effect on restructuring not only the individuals' sense of personal meaning and values, but the institution's values as well.

> *"People in my client organizations are forming small spiritual groups. They are praying together, they are getting together to talk about their lives, they are reading sacred texts together. These are not necessarily sanctioned by the authority of the corporation. But this is the way that spirituality is emerging in the work world today, primarily outside the official structures. Groups like this are just sprouting up all over the place."*[38]

The real yet largely unnoticed movement in our institutions involves the small spiritual group. These modest little community conversations can be enormously helpful, people tell us, in both doing the work of prolonging life, getting the corporation to run better, but also making life more satisfying and meaningful. As de Tocqueville long ago observed, Americans are the original self-help culture. When Americans have a problem, he noticed, they get together to solve the problem. This instinct is being applied to the problem of revitalizing our institutions. And it seems to be helping.

Notes — Chapter VIII

[1]   Arthur Waskow
[2]   For a discussion of this principle, see Owen Chadwick, *The Reformation* (NY: Pelican Books, 1964), p. 143.
[3]   Christopher Shaefer, "Applied Contemplative Disciplines in Work and Organizational Life" a High Tor Alliance report for Fetzer Foundation, 1996.
[4]   James Berry and Christopher Shaefer both note this. Note however that these claims are merely unconfirmed self reports, and notoriously unreliable.
[5]   David Wick
[6]   Richard Barrett.
[7]   PB
[8]   John Thompson, talk, "Spirituality in Business" at the Spirituality in Business conference, Mazatlan, Mexico, November, 1996.
[9]   Glenna Gerard
[10]   James Berry
[11]   Sharon Connelly
[12]   Martin Rutte
[13]   Martin Rutte
[14]   James Berry, paraphrasing Martin Rutte. This is a striking parallel to the old indentured servant or feudal lord and serf system. There too the notion was, I'll devote my life to you and you'll protect me in times of strife and trial. Just as the feudal lords ultimately let down the serfs, so too the General Motors and Raytheon corporations are letting down their employees.
[15]   James Berry
[16]   According to James Berry.
[17]   This is a theme of a recent *Journal of Consciousness Studies* issue, "Cognitive Models and Spiritual Maps", which Dr. Forman co-edited.
[18]   BL
[19]   Sigmund Freud, *Introductory Lectures in Psychoanalysis,* trans. J. Trachley, (NY: W.W. Norton, 1920).
[20]   Franz Alexander, *Psychosomatic Medicine: Its Principles and Applications* (New York: Norton, 1950).
[21]   Ron Anderson
[22]   Robin Norcross
[23]   Julie Mott
[24]   Ron Anderson

[25] Robin Norcross. See here Robert Jonas's moving account of
      his struggle to make sense of this situation, in *Rebecca: A
      Father's Journey* (New York: Crossroads, 1995).
[26] HB
[27] HB
[28] D Eisenberg, R.C. Kessler, C. Foster, F. Norlock, et al.
      "Unconventional Medicine in the United States: Preva-
      lence, Costs and Patterns of Use," *New England Journal of
      Medicine*, 1993, #328, pp. 246–252.
[29] Roger Booth
[30] Roger Booth
[31] BL
[32] BL
[33] Dean Ornish, S. Brown, L. Scherwitz, J Billings, W.
      Armstrong, T. Ports, S. McClanahan, R. Kirkeide, R. Brand
      and K. Gould, "Can Lifestyle Changes Reverse Coronary
      Artery Disease? The Lifestyle Heart Trial," *The Lancet*,
      #336, 1990, pp. 129–133.
[34] David Spiegel, H. Bloom, J. Kraemer, and F. Gottheil,
      "Effect of Psychosocial Treatment on Survival of Patients
      with Metastic Breast Cancer," *The Lancet*, # 335, 1989, pp.
      888–90.
[35] This is the conclusion one reaches from reading the High
      Tor Alliance's report. See Christopher Shaefer, "Applied
      Contemplative Disciplines in Work and Organizational
      Life," a report for Fetzer Foundation, 1996, p. 12.
[36] Glenna Gerard
[37] DF
[38] Diana Whitney

Chapter IX

Organizing the Un-Organizable

If I see you, I will laugh out loud
   or fall silent
   or explode into a thousand pieces.
If I don't see you I will
   be caught in the cement and stone
   of my own prison.

Rumi[1]

Grassroots Spirituality is an enormous movement. In sheer numbers, it dwarfs any denomination, most religions, and nearly every social movement of the past century. Its members are educated, comparatively wealthy, and in positions of importance.

And yet, oddly, most of its members feel painfully alone. We heard this plaint over and over.

> *"I have been teaching meditation, leading groups, working on my issues and yet it sometimes feels like I'm the only one doing this work. And yet I don't want to go back to the groupthink of my youth."* [2]

> *"I wish we could create community among those of us who are spiritual. We all feel that need, I think, we're all lonely."*[3]

*"It's important to be a part of a group in the spiritual life.
I felt that I had no help when I started meditating. There
were no books, and I was not attracted to someone like a
guru. It was very lonely. That's probably appropriate,
but it was lonely. I wanted to find people who were doing
the same thing."*[4]

A second problem was also named over and over. People in the spirituality world feel surprisingly powerless. Many of our interviewees mentioned that the alienation, self-aggrandizement and materialism of society have continued unabated. They feel like their efforts have been a "drop in the bucket." They often told us that they have felt relatively powerless to bring the deeper values they've discovered to society.

These two dots, of course, are connected. The absence of community, the loneliness and the lack of natural ways to find each another have stood in the way of these people finding each other and creating venues for long term cooperation. Though leaders of the Grassroots Spirituality Movement have spoken on panels together, cooperated on documentaries and met at many conferences, these contacts have given birth to surprisingly few long-term projects.

I often think of these spiritual leaders and teachers as a bit like cockroaches. Each leader has his or her students or disciples. But each group is running in their separate direction. Though, as we've seen, they all stand for something similar, their energies are scattered.

No wonder that this movement's effects on our larger society have been so muted!

Forming Communities around the Ineffable

What, we wonder, can be done to foster community that would be satisfying to these good hearted people? How might these folks better support each other's growth and help each other bring out the spirituality they've been fostering? How might they find natural ways to amplify their effect on society?

Here I must note that our interviewees did not have the answers. They — or I'll say "we" here — are all feeling our way into the unknown. For we have no models for successfully creating such an infrastructure. We face a challenge — of somehow bringing together spiritual leaders, teachers and adepts from every spiritual path and commitment — that human civilization has never successively accomplished. So in what follows, you will see both the insights of our interviewees and my own tentative ideas. I must take off the "just a researcher" hat, and become a participant observer, offering my own thoughts and ideas along with those of others.

Towards the end of our interviews, we asked our informants to brainstorm with us about what they thought might help enhance the broad spirituality world. We asked some, "what would you like to see happen to enhance the world of spirituality?" or "what would help you in your spiritual work?" Sometimes we asked, seemingly tongue in cheek, "if you had a million dollars and wanted to make spirituality grow and thrive, what would you do with it?"

There were certainly a healthy range of suggestions, which we'll highlight below. Several were highly skeptical of the whole idea: "*a million dollars would do nothing. People have to come to this place of knowing by themselves.*"[5]

But most did have suggestions, many of them intriguing. As was true elsewhere in our research, what surprised us the most about their opinions was their consistency. Almost universally, we heard one suggestion over and over. People said something like, "you know, a community, with small groups, ongoing conversations among spiritually dedicated people, in which we could all just talk about our lives and work and think together about the future, would be really helpful."

"Let's create a space where organic spiritual values can emerge. We'll bring in more and more people for this process of dialogue and mutual growth. Little by little, we expand our groups to include more. We'll dialogue and taste each other's worldview and experiences and grow together. I think there needs to be a space, a community. I don't mean a new religion. I'm imagining a space where values like diversity and growth and openness can be cultivated."

"We should organize dialogues between diverse groups: sharing, for example, Sufi and Jewish stories. These should offer real dialogue on some subject — sharing stories together, praying together, whatever."[6]

"It is helpful to all see ourselves as tzizes, fringes, corners of a garment, and to see others in this world as fringes also. That is, to communicate with people from other traditions could help us break down the barriers. We could see what we share. For example is meditation something that we share? Is Quaker silence different from my silence? Are there common practices? This could be an exploration with others. And it would be good for this to happen on an ongoing basis."[7]

"The idea here is to create a community among those who are leading the spiritual groups, spiritual peer groups."[8]

Some of our informants imagined that these trans-traditional groups might be able to hatch out ideas about spirituality's future. But even more of them felt that the act of bringing together people from a variety of spiritual pathways would be *valuable in itself*. Again and again we heard folks tell us how much they have enjoyed exploring with other dedicated spiritual souls, and how much they would like to do it more:

"I would really like to have dialogue with people that are doing similar work but not in my traditions."

Sufi Suhrawardi Gebel put this particularly poetically:

"I was in one of these little groups once. We were all from the Northeast. There was a Christian, a Zen Buddhist and some other sort of Buddhist; several Christians and leaders of other sorts. At the beginning of the weekend we gave a public talk, but then we just met for the rest of the weekend. And it was wonderful. We felt that we were all treading the same kind of path, and that we shared a sacred atmosphere."[9]

Martin Rutte, a leader of the spirituality in business world was equally poetic about his experience in such gatherings, *"I just like to marinate in that atmosphere . . ."*[10]

Many of our respondents said that simply knowing that they are not alone could itself be enormously uplifting and therapeutic. *"Good friends who understand the way I feel about things are very helpful to my spiritual life."*[11] We are able to learn from the others' insights and issues, share difficulties, share struggles and accomplishments.

Thus people told us loud and clear what would help: *"I think that there is a deep spiritual need for a real sense of community."*[12]

Since conducting our interviews, several groups have begun to bring spiritual people together and to begin to form loose and network-oriented organization to this far flung community. "Contemplative Mind in Society" has brought together people who have been teaching meditation and contemplation, especially in association with college classes. Though the groups have reportedly been dominated by Buddhists, they have invited teachers of Christian, Hindu and other forms of contemplation.[13]

The Fetzer Institute, which funded the research for the book, has been bringing together spiritual teachers, educators and other groups, but on a short term, week or weekend long basis.

The Integral Institute, founded by Ken Wilber, tried to bring Wilber's vast vision to life by bringing together people in a range of fields who support his Integral (all quadrants / all levels / all lines) worldview. For several years Wilber brought some of the finest integrally oriented minds together to begin to manifest this view in communities around the country.

Education as Transformation, housed in Wellesley College, has formed a diverse network of educators who are trying to bring higher values and spirituality to the college community. They have sponsored several conferences and are tying people together via a periodic e-newsletter.

Finally The Forge Institute, of which both of our authors are members and Dr. Forman is CEO, has been building long term, local communities of spiritual leaders and teachers of every stripe. This organization, the Forge Guild of trans-traditionally oriented spiritual leaders and teachers, brings together not only meditation teachers and clergy men and women, but also writers, spiritual psychologists and other specialists in chapters around the United States, Canada and Europe. While the Forge Guild is a professional organization for the movement's leadership, the Forge Institute has also begun ongoing yet diverse communities that will help the seeking "public" come together across paths and traditions.

These and similar efforts seem to be offering just the kind of loose and network-oriented communities that our interviewees longed for. (Indeed, The Forge Institute's efforts grew out of this research.) From all reports, these efforts seem to be bearing important fruit.

Why is that, and where do these efforts seem to be heading?

The Conditions for Healthy, Non-dogmatic Communities

We have stressed the remarkable similarity in what we heard from our interviewees. Such parallels in basic attitude and life commitment may turn out to be key to these efforts. For the parallels we heard so clearly can be heard as well by others.

At the basis of mutual spiritual exploration is trust. In order to explore at the depths, participants need to sense that those with whom they are exploring know intuitively of what they're speaking. The kind of common ground we have discovered may make just this kind of trust possible.

People in these grassroots explorations are discovering how much they may have in common. In small groups, weekend gatherings, one on one conversations, and even in larger groups, the sense of a "panentheistic" one is often being discovered and used as a common ground. And from what we have seen, it can make healthy spiritual conversation possible.

My first experience of this sort happened when I attended a weekend retreat with a handful of spiritual leaders and teachers from a range of traditions. There were about 15 men and women on the retreat. Most were on paths different than my own: there were Catholics, a Tibetan meditator, a Christian professor of theology, a spiritual psychologist and a protestant minister. As we told our stories it was soon clear to us all that we all knew and are dedicated to a similar way of being alive. Through all of our stories we heard of lives centered on silence, the experience of a presence or a sense of emptiness that ran through the world and within the speaker, and a commitment to ongoing growth. As we listened to each other's spiritual struggles and could sense the depths of each person's experience, I felt that we were sometimes able to drop down beneath our words and differences into some vast communal spaciousness.

To me it sometimes seemed like a group mystical experience. Inviting each other into that silence, letting go of our judgments about each other, we just held each other in that space and listened deeply. We talked of our hurts, loves, concerns, successes or failings. The subject didn't seem to really matter. Instead, we just became more awake

to the depths we shared, to each other in his or her struggles, and to being in that presence.

Others have felt that common silence as well. Elisabeth
Ursic, a Catholic lay leader from Arizona, describes her
experience of this kind of contact with two spiritually oriented men, neither a Catholic, in the Forge.

> *"I had come together with two men to discuss spiritual
> facilitation and spiritual direction work. I had even
> brought handouts, ready for a typical meeting.*
>
> *But at some point in the meeting our interaction spon-
> taneously shifted. It was like we dropped down together
> into something deeper. We became quieter, more present,
> aware of a certain presence among us. It was palpable
> enough that we collectively noticed and commented on it.
> In fact we found this new way of being together much
> more interesting than the ideas we had been discussing.
> As we continued talking we all felt a greater openness
> and honesty between us that seemed connected to what
> we were experiencing.*
>
> *We continued our discussion even while we were with
> each other in this deeper place. Our personalities and per-
> spectives were intact yet we were communally nurturing
> a deeper spiritual movement at the same time. I physi-
> cally felt my heart open. In some ways it was involun-
> tary. I felt myself wanting to receive and contribute to
> this gift. And it was a gift."*[14]

Susan Quinn, a Jewish and Zen leader and organizational consultant, writes of a similar experience during a
weekend workshop of people in the Forge Guild from a
range of spiritual pathways:

> *"Early in the workshop, we divided into groups of three.
> Our purpose: to share of our experiences of the transcen-
> dent. Two of the participants asked to work with me,
> since they knew me the least of the entire group. One of
> them suggested I go first. Instead of feeling put on the*

spot, I felt invited to the dance. I immediately felt the genuine curiosity and caring of both men as I began to articulate a sincere and relevant answer.

Throughout my sharing, and as both men shared their stories, a palpable energy was created. It was as if we were not only inviting each other to share, but another force had joined us, or had been created, that took us beyond our stories and manifested a new story, our new story as dedicated spiritual seekers and friends. Time left us alone.

At the same time, as a person who can sometimes be guarded and skeptical, I felt my own growth in my willingness to trust and disclose.

Our backgrounds in faith had both similarities and differences, our stories were deep, mystical, personal and genuine, and we all seemed to connect to each others' tales. We seemed to transcend any particularities of our practices, and were fostering our own way of being in those heartfelt moments. As our knowledge of each other expanded through our sharing, intimacy grew, and there was a sense of spaciousness, openness and freedom to be, just as we were. As the bell was rung to end our sharing, I knew we had planted the seeds of friendship and reinforced the commitment to our mission."[15]

It seems clear that what I and these others are finding is that our deep spiritual experiences and commitments are indeed surprisingly common. We all shared a sense of silence and spaciousness. We all shared the human struggle to let go of our clingings, and to stretch and grow. While Hindus, Catholics, Buddhists and Jews may refer to it differently, we've all seen that in these moments of intimate sharing, we can sometimes *sense* together our common ground.

"It is good to be with people in that communal silence. It is good to know others are there. It deepens my commitment. There is a firmness in that supportive energy."[16]

And Evelyn Brush, we saw, stated;

> *"A spiritual community can help me to see what I believe and experience it mirrored in others. In our writing community, for example, this is strong. It's a sense of grace — that when I'm together with them something has been altered and multiplied in me and in the world. It's a kind of spiritual energy. I feel physically and emotionally different in community. When we sing, walk, meditate or are in silence, things are more aligned within me, like a compass. [It helps me] have a felt sense of this connection to something larger."*[17]

Thus the experience of what we have called the panentheistic one seems to provide some common ground, the sense that what we're really after is similar. Such a common ground seems to make it possible not only to communicate with each other though our paths are diverse, but to really deepen and learn with each other.

That sense of deep connection with others is another leitmotif. Elizabeth said,

> *"as we continued talking we all felt a greater openness and honesty between us that seemed connected to what we were experiencing."* Susan wrote: *"as our knowledge of each other expanded through our sharing, intimacy grew, and there was a sense of spaciousness, openness and freedom to be, just as we were. . . I knew we had planted the seeds of friendship."*

There seems to be something about these experiences of sharing among folks from different spiritual paths that fosters particularly deep intimacy. Here we have reports of people coming together from diverse traditions. Their language and assumptions are different. Their styles of being spiritual are different. And yet they are building a special kind of intimacy.

Why? I believe that coming together across differences may be the very reason *that* they are finding these conversations and experiences especially valuable. For those very differences may serve as catalysts to foster ever deeper experiences of the infinite.

When we come together with spiritual people with whom we share a path or a set of beliefs, we unconsciously assume a great deal in common. A meditator with his meditating friends or a Catholic with her Catholic buddies share uncountable assumptions about the right way or style of being spiritual. Because they share so many assumptions with their mates, it is easy for each to avoid challenging or questioning those assumptions. Yet what Catholic, Buddhist and Sufis are all *really* tapping into is not the terms or the assumptions. What they're actually after, they know, is that ineffable one that is beyond all of their words.

To be with people who don't share one's assumptions or beliefs can serve as a kind of irritant, causing us to reflect on and reach past our assumed truths. When I was on that Forge retreat I mentioned, a Catholic spiritual director spoke about working on her "growing edge." Now that sounds innocent enough, but my TM training stressed that we were not to "work" on our spiritual issues, but that the meditation practices would effortlessly take care of them. Inside I struggled with that phrase "growing edge."

But after a while, I realized that I did indeed have lots of areas in my life I was actively working on, and they were important to my spiritual life. I was working on my psychological issues, on my marriage, on the ways to think about spirituality, and on and on. In coming to terms with her phrase, I had to let go of an assumption about spirituality and open my door another notch. Her language, which came out of her background, had served as a goad for me to keep stretching.

I often find that exploring with folks who have different orientations helps me expand the way I think of my life and address my issues. Folks on paths other than my own have helped me understand the sense of quiet commitment I feel, the devotion in my heart, how I am relating to my wife and my friends, what happens when I become anxious, and how all this connects to my body. Exploring with others who do *not* share my path and assumptions is a rich delight, for my life has been endlessly enriched by their unexpected approaches and their wisdom.

The common spiritual ground allows us to communicate; the differences help stimulate us to grow.

The point is that when spiritual people come together with others who are *not* on their path and yet who share a similar sense of the sacred, it soon becomes obvious that that there are other ways to relate with the infinite, and that it is not my words or my way but the *infinite* that we're all after. It becomes obvious that my favorite way of talking is but one way of many. And it becomes clear that I have a great deal to learn. Seeing the sanity of another's way of being spiritual helps us each let go a notch. And that, after all, is what the spiritual path is all about.

I for one don't know another way to achieve this kind of letting go even beyond my own assumptions about the path than by coming together with other sincere seekers who are different yet with whom I share at the depths.

If we remain alone, or always hang out with people who share our worldview or our "style" of being spiritual (intuitive, intellectual, bodily, etc.) we'll never be challenged enough that we can see our worldview as just a view.

Many people have bemoaned the fact that in our pluralistic society we have lost our common values and assumptions. There are no longer any common values, suggest some on the right, and we need to reinstate them, by law if necessary.

But herein may lay the amazing opportunity of pluralism. By coming together with a sense of a common ground with folks from paths unlike our own, we can more easily come to see that our way is but one way, our style but one style. It can challenge us to let go of our attachments to our way. By the way, it doesn't mean we will be forced to *let go of* our way. Not at all. The Christian who undergoes this process will remain a Christian, the Jew a Jew. But they may become more self- reflective in their paths, and be more able to see that it's not the path they value so but that to which the path is pointing.

For this process, we at the Forge have coined the term: "*trans-traditional.*" By trans-traditional I mean that we hold ourselves and our paths in the light of our common spiritual depths, that we recognize that those depths challenge us to keep growing within and possibly beyond any single path, and that we come together across paths to sense our common ground while at the same time exploring our differences.

I believe that such *trans-traditional spirituality* is just what our pluralistic grassroots community needs. It would be wonderful if people were to systematically come together, willing to explore their common spiritual ground and use their very differences to encourage further discovery. I believe that held aright, our differences could not only cause us all to learn, but also challenge those in the Grassroots Spirituality Movement to actualize that spiritual ground more and more deeply.

If we can discover that common ground, and hold each other in its breadth, our communities may find new and exciting ways to come together across our ancient differences.

Vive la difference!

Organizing Trans-traditional Processes

Robert Wuthnow, student of small groups, points out that in general spiritual groups do not just happen. If the Grassroots Spiritual Community is to come together more effectively than hitherto, there needs to be some sort of organized efforts, even if low key. Someone needs to arrange locations, get the word out, help people find each other and come together, arrange for the coffee pot, and train the facilitators that can help keep conversations productive.[18] Somebody needs to begin the process.

What kind of processes? Here again, we heard a fair amount of agreement:

• **Processes should be intimate**

First, there was general agreement that for conversations to go into the kind of depth sharing we've just heard about, the groups should remain small. Most felt that some number between 10 and 15 should be the maximum.

> *"I'd like to see groups, say 6–16, to be able to get to know each other. If it's larger, it gets too diffuse, no one gets to say much, or it gets hierarchical, where some get to speak for 30 minutes, or the few talkers take over."*

Anything larger than 15 tends to become a mini-conference or a lecture, which our respondents felt unlikely to foster the kind of personal and intimate group exploration they longed for.

> *"Instead of the mega-conferences, I think that small local meetings can be most helpful."*[19]

> *"Most productive would be to create opportunities for all of us to be in dialogue with each other. Small groups of maybe 25 tops."*[20]

If however a community is to get larger, as many long for, how can this spirit of intimacy be maintained? Several people have mentioned the power of breaking a large body into smaller dialogue groups — of three, of five or six or the like. Kay Lindahl in California told us of a huge gathering she hosted. She broke several hundred into small groups and invited them to dialogue deeply on a particular subject. After some time, some of the people from each table migrated to other tables, thus communicating around the room the insights of each small circle and sharing with each.

Many we have spoken with tell us of the power of breaking a large group into intimate groups of 3 or 4. After participants have a deep experience in that intimate setting, they can bring their insights and questions back to the larger group. Thus the quality of intimacy is be maintained while still forming larger communities.

These creative ideas and others like them may serve to help this grassroots community gather together here and there on a long term basis while still maintaining the level of intimacy and authentic sharing that its members so crave.

• Conversations should be non-dogmatic

We heard over and over that these conversations must be non-dogmatic. People have had it with dogma and pressure to conform; that was eminently clear. There can be no dictated beliefs, no catechisms, and no bars to free exploration. *"This is not a dogmatic vision of the answer or even the process."*[21]

People in this movement want to be able to share their stories, explore their problems, celebrate their joys and successes, and rethink their spirituality with no hierarchical authorities telling them what to believe or feel. What these folks seem to crave is real and sincere dialogue, open, honest and heartfelt. *"It can only be helpful if all the parties are willing to let go of their own way and learn from the others. Real dialogue means dropping the grip of my language, dogma and expectations."*[22] "It is not the seeking after God that divides, but the claim to have found God."[23]

Perhaps the one dictum might be: *thou shalt not try to convert!*

• Local ongoing gatherings

The spirituality community has been blessed with many, many fine speakers and excellent weekend workshops.

These have been valuable. But people are hungry, we have heard from countless people, for community. For explorations to really dig into one's harder spiritual material, they must be long term and regular. Infrequent retreats rarely form true communities. For participants to really explore in depth, they must be local and ongoing. Community is not built in a weekend, but week after week.

• **Local conversations with national infrastructure**

And yet people need to know that they are part of a large scale, globe-wide community. Part of the problem in the Grassroots Spirituality Movement is that people feel alone, as if they are the only ones involved in spirituality. It would be profoundly encouraging to know that someone in, say, a Dallas group is not alone in their commitment to spiritual exploration and a life of depth. It would be encouraging to know that there are healthy spirituality groups in New York, Barcelona and Toronto, and that they're engaging in similar struggles.

This means that any local or regional small groups should be structured in such a way that they know they are part of and can feed back into a larger society-wide dialogue. That larger nation-wide process might in turn feed issues, processes and ideas back to the local explorations and common effort. A newsletter, web page or other communications channels could bring home to all involved that they are all engaged in a very wide and important conversation that may very well influence our civilization.

Obviously some communications network would be needed to make it possible for people to learn from each other's successes, mistakes and failures, and to possibly work in common.

Thus local community forums can serve several interrelated functions at once:

  • personal satisfaction for the participants;

- support of the individual within the group;
- mutual support of each person's spiritual work in the world
- enhancement of the local community;
- input into the broader national and international conversations;
- weaken the hold of old dogmatic ways of thinking;
- developing a new common language;
- help enable both individuals and the group to open to the wider spirit.

Structure the Process, Not the Content

We want to stress this last point. Spiritual process, and spiritual communities, must have some structure, people agreed. But their emphasis should be on healthy process, not on the control of belief or of faith content.

For such trans-traditional processes to be helpful, they must help participants dig into their depths. It is easy to skirt on the surface. Several suggested that we should turn to the best facilitators we know to build a set of tools that help foster truly rich explorations.

As part of this research project, we contacted several such people. A number of them offered a few helpful guidelines about engendering productive dialogues. Here are some of the groundrules we heard. We offer them not as fixed catechism but as merely a start:

1. Healthy communication involves real listening, *the ability to develop a witness without reaction*.[24] Dialogue won't work if one has to defend one's turf, for people won't be able to really hear each other. Each will be determined to make his or her own views known.

"Real dialogue is not about talking. If someone really opens up, then both learn from it. It's about really listening. It can only be helpful if all the parties are willing to let go of their own way and learn from the others."[25]

We can call this "dialogic" as opposed "dialectic" communication, in which one party tries to refute the claims of the other. In dialogic communication (1) each partner meets the other in an atmosphere of mutual understanding and (2) each partner is mutually enriched by passing over into the consciousness of the other so that each can experience the other's values from within the other's perspective. It is important to respect the autonomy of the other tradition. This means grounding ourselves in our own traditions yet at the same time opening ourselves to the other.[26]

2. Healthy communication stresses telling the truth, sincerely and fully. That means it must foster a sense of exploration within an atmosphere of trust, or, as one put it, exploring the edges of what we already know...

   "I try to create an environment in which people feel free to express themselves and tell the truth. If we create the proper environment, people will bring all of themselves to the table.

   The purpose of the group is to assist each other in honestly probing and addressing personal issues which can interfere with or enhance the individual's response to their life issues."[27]

3. Effective spiritual groups are not advice groups. Unless someone specifically asks for advice, participants should refrain from offering it. Rather they are places for each person to hear each other deeply and to respond to each others' explorations, questions and insights with an openness and honesty which bares vulnerability in a real way.[28] They are to touch on

exploratory questions, unacknowledged assumptions, and unrecognized truths.

"What helps the spiritual life? Vulnerability and a willingness to really feel the opposites. What helps one become vulnerable? The safety of trusting environments. This cannot be done alone. It is best done with others."[29]

4. Healthy groups can use a variety of means, verbal and non verbal, rational and non rational, at different times. Everyone has their own practices, so the sensitive facilitator should allow each group to find and use whatever practices might help. In addition to verbal explorations, one might use contemplative prayer, a movement exercise, or pray to be grateful for what is. Other groups might use mandalas, mantras, whirling, walking, singing, sitting attentively, etc.

5. Healthy communities share an attitude of commitment. Whether the agreement is for 30 weeks, a quarter or a year, it should be clear that those who choose to participate will be faithful to the group, and commit to be there at all regularly scheduled meetings. Groups tend to straggle if they end up with a "drop in when you can" attitude. The leader of the group should state and insist on the nature of this commitment from the very start.[30]

6. Healthy groups hold each other accountable. It's easy to pretend that everything is all right, that we can go along with anything, no matter what. But once the commitment becomes solid, members of healthy groups will hold each other accountable to their (the doer's) highest values. This demands responsibility and trust.

7. Healthy communities should always remain open to becoming more than mere self-help and mutual support groups. There should be an openness to the group's taking on sort of common activity, outreach or

projects, such as helping others develop spiritually or embarking on a service project.

"Some of the spirituality I see in the Grassroots Spirituality World is disconnected from others. If [spirituality] is to be real it must have an effect on others."[31]

8. These small groups should meet, as we said, with the understanding that they are part of a society-wide, national and global exploration of spirituality. As such, they should be attentive to projects that are coming up elsewhere, and without being slavish be open to taking on appropriate endeavors.

"The group process can and should get to the meaning dimension in the local area, and also into the meta dialogue. It needs to explore what are the values implicit in the process? In a discussion of the process, a discussion of values will grow. It is implicit, and should be made explicit. That is, what are the beliefs that lead into this particular articulation of a process? The model here is that insight will flow from the individual to the group to the larger group as well as the other way."[32]

The organizers of this nation-wide process must walk a fine line here. Healthy, society-wide dialogues cannot be overly regulated, for this will deaden the group dynamic. But nor can the process be utterly without vision or direction. It is well-known that leaderless groups or groups without an overarching agenda tend to fizzle out. According to Robert Wuthnow's surveys, 90% of American small groups have a leader, and 84% have a stated goal. Psychologist Arthur Deikman suggests that every healthy spiritual group must have a task.[33]

In facilitating such a process, its organizers will need to be a midwife for the process itself, allowing it to shape itself naturally yet invisibly, so it can find, form and give birth to itself. Its leaders must never forget, they are not the doers here, but rather the midwives for something much larger than they.

Thus any organization that develops to help engender this process should be systematic but not heavy-handed, visionary but not demagogic, both male and female.

The Spirituality of Trans-traditional Groups

The kind of trans-traditional exploration that has been dawning in this Grassroots Spirituality Movement is in alignment with its fundamental calling. For the explorations that we are witnessing seek to be aimed at reaching towards the depths of openness and honesty. One woman who participated in one such conversation at the Forge Institute told us of her experience when Sarah spoke. Sarah was at a crossroads, trying to decide whether to become a minister of her church or to go and live with her elderly French boyfriend.

"I was so moved by Sarah's account," she said, *"because she was being honest about something that really mattered to her. I was moved also by the other people in the Forge group. Not one person jumped in to say 'do this or do that.' Their questions were all about 'how are you responding?' or 'here's what I hear you saying.' We were all very sympathetic to her plight, even though many of us, like me, wouldn't have had a problem like that, since we aren't involved in the church. Yet no one was even tempted to say, 'What, are you crazy?' We all just sat with her and listened because she was expressing herself and her dilemma so honestly. We were all allowing her to express and do whatever she needed. Despite the fact that our conditions and beliefs were, on the surface, so different, we were all utterly sympathetic to her plight. The connection and the helpfulness came from both the honesty of her depiction and from the clarity she could achieve because we all listened and cared so much."*[34]

It is just this sort of dynamic, sympathetic, open dialogue process that people seem to long for. They stress not answering but rather ongoing questioning and exploring. Because people come from a range of beliefs and approaches, no one comes with a position of dogmatic certainty, but rather with the humility of exploration. Participants thus remain open to change and reflection.

Here's how such a process is in accord with the very spirituality it is to support:

1. Open exploration helps each person actually connect with what is larger: not only his or her group, but also the dynamic, society-wide whole and the expansive spirit. In effect, as one of our respondents said, open mutual exploration is "walking the talk."

2. It is fundamentally egalitarian, as is the Grassroots Spirituality movement as a whole. *Non*-hierarchical to the core, it invites openness and connections.

3. To bring together spiritual people of a variety of beliefs, it is clear that there will be neither firmly fixed dogmas nor catechisms. This is in full harmony with the thrust of Grassroots Spirituality. In its emphasis on spiritual exploration, the process will remain open to the unknown and the not-strictly-rational. Spiritual dialogue can push us through the envelope of our certainties, and thus enhances our exploration into the *un*certain.

   There is neither need nor interest in *imposing* any beliefs on the process. While we have already noted much "theological" agreement among our respondents, that was a descriptive, not a prescriptive agreement. Any healthy dialogue process should be just that, a dialogue between people of admittedly different opinions and beliefs. Thus the process should remain inherently non-dogmatic.

4. When you enter into contact with that deeper Self, you begin to deepen your connections with it. Your under-

standing, your values, and your tasks will inevitably change. And you yourself will be changed by that contact. As the Sri Lankan saying has it, "we build the road, but the road builds us."[35] For example, in the act of honoring what is most authentic in ourselves, we are shaped by that honoring. This *is* spiritual work.

Spiritual transformation can certainly happen alone, as we know. But it happens in different ways within a group and relationships. The process of articulating one's understanding, experiences and feelings to one another can itself be extremely freeing. One of the lessons of psychotherapy is that when you are finally able to articulate "what you really feel," it can be extremely healing. The deeper you go into what you have experienced, the deeper can be the healing. Small, spiritual exploration groups can offer a forum in which people can say what they really feel and think. That itself is spiritually and psychologically evolutionary.

5. Participation in such groups represents a spiritual maturity rarely seen in any other gathering. For many years spiritual people have participated in their groups, talked to people on their own paths, learned from their comrades. A lot have gotten stuck there, we heard, and never do overcome the naive thought that their way is the only way, their theology the only true one. But the trans-traditional spiritual dialogue process calls for and engenders a new level of spiritual maturity. It marks being ready to be open to and to learn from people who have learned to cherish other truths.

This is not like being on "my" path and learning from it. Nor is it merely like being on my path and seeing that there are other paths. Rather it is being on a path and recognizing that people on other paths *really can* help and teach me. It forces each of us to acknowledge that even though someone may be on a different path than we are, they may be able to hold my hand, toss me a rope, and help me see through my blind spots. And that, despite the fact that they don't do what I think humans "should," they can be wise. Such humility is the sign of and helps foster true spiritual maturity, for it implies that "we," whoever "we" may be, do not have an exclusive grip on the right way or the truth. It marks an acceptance of our own foolishness, and a coming of age of the arrogance of exclusivist spiritualities.

In short real spiritual growth can emerge from being with people on other paths. To learn from another, to discover their truth, to add it to my own, and to empathize with another — these all promise real expansion, real spiritual growth.

We believe that long term spiritual adepts, the kind of people we interviewed, are the most prepared to conduct such mature spiritual dialogues. But this possibility is not beyond any group, if they come into it with the right attitude.

Notes — Chapter IX

[1] Recited to us by Angela Arrien
[2] RKC
[3] Stuart Smithers
[4] SE
[5] Susan Izard
[6] Tony Stern
[7] Arthur Waskow
[8] Stuart Smithers
[9] Suhrawardi Gebel
[10] Martin Rutte
[11] Christian Peck
[12] MT
[13] Ed Sarath, a member of this community, mentioned the Buddhist domination in a private conversation.
[14] *Forge Guild Newsletter*, Vol 4, no. 3.
[15] Susan Quinn, Forge Guild Listserve, Jan 03.
[16] KS
[17] Evelyn Brush
[18] Robert Wuthnow, *Sharing the Journey*, pp. 89-119.
[19] Suhrawardi Gebel
[20] Glenna Gerard
[21] Glenna Gerard
[22] Janet Abels
[23] Mordechai Kaplan, quoted by Joshua Hammerman "On One Foot; A Rabbi's Journal."
[24] Glenna Gerard
[25] Janet Abels
[26] Paraphrased from Ewert Cousins, *Christ of the Twenty First Century*, p. 9.
[27] Felicia McKnight, "Group Spiritual Direction: Intentionality and Diversity," *Presence*, Vol. 1, no. 3, (Sept. 1995), pp. 29–44.
[28] Paraphrased from Mary Ellen Murphy, in McKnight, *Group Spiritual Direction: Intentionality and Diversity*.
[29] Felicia McKnight
[30] Paraphrased from Felicia McKnight's *Group Spiritual Direction*.
[31] MI
[32] Paraphrased from Jeremy Waletzky.
[33] Robert Wuthnow, *Sharing the Journey* (New York: Free Press, 1994), p. 135.
[34] Rachel Harris
[35] Quoted by Sharif Abdullah.

Chapter X

What Can We Do Together?

There is a fundamental misconception among spiritual people that, oh we should just go with the flow. We are co-creators in this spiritual process. We should be as actively engaged in life as we would like the creator to be. Spirituality is not a path of withdrawal or apathy. It calls us to be fully engaged with life. You should know when it is time to withdraw and when it is time to engage.

Diana Whitney

The Three Great Challenges of the Grassroots Spirituality Movement

Spirituality does not mean merely going with the flow: Applied spirituality involves work, thought and all the energy we can muster.

"We are co-creators in the growth of spirit. The minister in my church used to say, we should live as if it's all up to God, and we should work as if it's all up to us. There is a fundamental misconception among spiritual people that, oh we should just go with the flow. We are co-creators in this spiritual process. We should be as actively engaged in life as we would like the creator to be. Spirituality is not a path of withdrawal or apathy. It calls us to be fully

*engaged with life. You should know when it is time to
withdraw and when it is time to engage.*"[1]

I believe that there are three great challenges that face
the Grassroots Spirituality Movement. Responding creatively to them will mean the difference between a movement that survives over the long term and one that is
merely a passing blip of history.

1. Can We Learn to Work Together?

I think Doug Kruschke laid down the first and probably
greatest challenge facing the Grassroots Spirituality
Movement:

> *"This is the grand project. It calls us all to grow up. That
> project is at the center of my life, of all of our lives I think.
> The grand project is not about getting wealthy, or being
> famous. It's about going beyond ego and getting in tune
> with the infinite beyond all our languages, our traditions
> and mostly all of our ego stuff. . . To be spiritually mature
> is to realize that there is no one language or conceptual
> system that can contain this. It has to be lived, though it
> is beyond one system. Our systems, if we think they're it,
> can become a block to this. They can block the flow of
> spirit. [But I think it is possible to] all live this way
> together. Now there's a grand project!"*[2]

Kruschke's challenge for this movement is, can we not
only learn to live these values ourselves? Can we discover
our common ground — the kind of experiential commonalities that we have articulated here — and live together in
its light? And if we can, can we work together to bring its
values to society?

So many souls are caught up in the quest for wealth,
fame, power and the like. As we have seen, the Grassroots
Spirituality Movement says that another set of values —
spiritual depth, value and meaning in life — are far more

important and life enhancing. The discovery and actualization of the single spiritual water table that hides beneath our separate lives and traditions offers a very different kind of value.

Many have taught that one can discover the sacred and live out its deeper values within the context of their chosen religious or spiritual path. But, Kruschke continues, this very thought can itself easily become a block to actualizing such deeper values. The spiritual leaders we spoke with tend to affirm his thought. No one path has a monopoly on the spirit, no single tradition is the only true way. Dogmatic certainty or even attachment to some one tradition or path can be a block to not only living together in harmony but also to fostering ongoing and open ended spiritual growth that is one of the hallmarks of a truly spiritual life.

Here then is the first and most important challenge facing this spiritual movement: Can we, its members, learn to live together across paths and traditions?

Doing so must be more than mere lip-service. It's one thing to *say* that no one path has the only truth. It's a whole other matter to actually talk, work and grow together spiritually. And it's again another matter to actually help each other bring out what we have in common, spiritual depths and the commitment to self reflection, to the seeking public.

It sounds almost strange to say it, but the first and truly most important challenge facing this movement is to "get itself together." How can we, its members, reach across our ancient divides and learn to cooperate, love and work together?

It will not be easy. Each path, each spiritual leader or teacher, loves his or her path or way of being spiritual. Many, I have sensed, want (secretly, unconsciously) to be the leader of this larger effort. But to come together we must all drop this particular fantasy, and be willing to let those secret drives go and learn to work well with others.

We must be creative enough to bring some infrastructure to this enormous movement, yet without sacrificing the freedom of choice and self determination that is so crucial to each of us, its members.

There is a great responsibility here. Virtually all of our interviewees *recognize* that the spirit that runs within their paths is much the same as the spirit that runs within the others. Virtually all say they recognize that their way is not the only or even necessarily the best way. Though members of this movement see this, can we actually live it?

Gandhi said, famously, that "you must become the change you wish to see in the world." Can the facilitators, clergy, meditation teachers and the members of this movement actually live this change, walk this talk? Can we work, meditate and bring about change in the world together in such a way that we are manifesting the very common ground that we wish to promote in society?

Doing so, I believe, should enhance each of our various paths, not destroy them. As we have seen, the process of exploring one's deepest concerns and experiences with sincere seekers from other paths can itself enhance our own search and our dedication to our own way. Perhaps this will be part of the logic of coming together.

Here's where the efforts of The Forge Institute, Contemplative Mind in Society, the Integral Institute, Fetzer Institute, "The Education as Transformation Project" and other similar organizations may be truly critical. They have each risen up to meet the challenge of bringing spiritual people from various traditions together.

2. Local Trans-Traditional Spirituality Centers

For long term survival, a community must have places and ways of gathering. People must be able to meet, congregate over the long term, and learn together. Singles must have ways to meet each other and young families must have ways to educate their children. For the teachings and wisdom that this movement values to survive long term, there must be some place or home within which its members can come together, teach and deepen their spiritual insights.

At present, there is no natural place for members of this extended movement to do this. Where can spiritual people naturally and regularly meet, explore their lives or their spiritual depths or to find other like-minded souls?

Places that have become this movement's foci are such centers as Eselen, Wainwright House in Rye, NY, the Open Center, Omega and local spiritual bookstores. They typically offer a range of lectures, workshops and other short term programs. But these places are not succeeding in meeting their constituent's needs. Notes Fordham professor Jack Healey,

> *"What's killing Interfaith, The Wainwright House and The Open center? Their problem is they have to make money. Thus their programs are market driven, and do not tend to develop a solid spirituality or spiritual community that will address real spiritual needs. Market driven means that bad money drives out the good: You'll always develop your stars, your crowd pleasers, and invite them back. These are not necessarily the best people, but rather celebrities. This plays to popular culture rather than developing a solid spirituality."*[3]

What Healey longs for is centers that offer truly authentic, long term spiritual growth, not just popular courses. *"It would be wonderful to have an endowed center that could be run cheaply and autonomously."*[4]

But there are no such autonomous homes. Spirituality has no place where people can explore subjects that matter to them on a long term basis with folks they've come to know well. Nor are there natural places for spiritual people to hear of and get involved with each other's service projects.

But can the members of the Grassroots Spirituality Movement create community homes for themselves? The key is that such homes must foster individual exploration and freedom of choice as well as ways to come together. But that, after all should not be impossible.

Given the world situation, this is no small matter. If we cannot learn to live together in a long term and loving way, we will continue to harm each other and even go to war with those on different pathways. The only long term solution I can think of is to find a way to bring together members of the full panoply of traditions and paths under a single spiritual roof. I can imagine few things more exciting than to see a rabbi, a priest, a minister and a Zen Roshi all intentionally holding their very different services, mentoring their very different congregations, in a single space. It would be an enormous leap for mankind if serious seekers from Buddhism, Taoism, Christianity and Sufism were all meeting and interacting with each other in the same spiritual center, and that they might find folks from almost any path who were interested in exploring with them in a non-evangelical way their spiritual lives and experiences.

What would it say to participants if they were to be in touch with clearly interesting and growing people who were on paths like and unlike their own? In such a context it would certainly be difficult to maintain the illusion that one's own path is necessarily the best, the fastest or the only way. This alone would go far towards helping people transcend the ancient enmities between our faiths and paths. It is hard to hate or war with folks on other paths if you have learned to love them.

This will not be easy. To create satisfying community centers of the spirit is, as one of our contacts recently put it, a non-trivial challenge.

And yet creating trans-traditional spiritual community centers that offer a range of spiritual teachings, facilities, mentors and partners may turn out to be one of the most exciting new possibilities for our society. For, once we in this vast movement, possibly a majority of the western world, learn to come and work together, there is no limit to we could accomplish. Why should our society remain forever in shallow, materialistic darkness?

3. New Ways of Addressing Social Problems

If this movement is to have an impact on society worthy of its size and importance, it will have to develop an approach to social issues that is consonant with its principles. Its members will have to develop new ways of thinking about and answering the pressing issues of the day. But what might that be?

Many people have assumed that members of the Grassroots Spirituality Movement would naturally be on the left side of the political spectrum. Spiritual people would tend to be pacifists, like the Quakers or Mennonites, or at least lean left. While we did not ask people of their political persuasions when we interviewed them, it is clear that members of this movement, scions of the sixties, tend to lean left. But that is *by no means consistent.* During discussions among spiritual leaders and teachers of my acquaintance during 2003 about the possibility of war with Iraq, I for one was surprised how *varied* and thoughtful the viewpoints were. Some participants were quite far on the right of the spectrum, others centrist, and many either left or far left.

I would suggest that if the Grassroots Spirituality Movement ever develops a voice in the public scene, it will not be a single viewpoint. This movement is far too varied to cherish a single viewpoint. For just as this movement cuts across religious and traditional lines, it cuts across traditional political lines as well. However, we have found no one on the radical right, which is associated with a religious view that is not open to or critical of other truths.

Rather than offering a single political viewpoint, I believe that the promise and challenge of the spirituality movement is to develop and bring to society new *processes* or *ways* of addressing our political issues. As we have seen, one of the leitmotifs of this movement is ongoing and open ended spiritual growth, be it through personal stretching or group work. When one comes up against a problem, our interviewees suggested, they take it as a challenge to listen, learn, stretch themselves and creatively come up with solutions. We heard several times that the word in Chinese for "obstacle" also means "opportunity." The Grassroots Spirituality Movement tends to sees possibility in seemingly intractable problems.

This attitude was particularly emphasized to us by spiritual people who specialize in dialogue, interpersonal and organizational work. They stressed that in listening deeply to others of different opinion, all parties can help each other discover what is really at issue, and together may be able to create solutions that work for all parties. The key is that instead of proving the other wrong, dialogue leaders encourage all parties to enter into the exploration with the assumption that the other is a reasonable human being, whose opinions and aspirations, even if different from one's own, are plausible and human. Even if we don't understand it at the outset, it is possible to *assume* that it makes some sense. To dig under presenting issues and to listen to what may be *really* at issue for people may lead to creative and mutual breakthroughs and co-creative solutions.

Here then is this movement's third challenge: to discover and encourage new means and tools in public dialogue that reaches beyond labeling or vilification of the opposite side of an issue. Can its members learn to use so called "obstacles" in our society like they use them in their own lives: seeing them as "opportunities." Can the members of the Grassroots Spirituality Movement somehow learn to listen to each others viewpoints on seemingly difficult issues in new ways. Can they not only listen well, but can they bring "opposing" sides together for brainstorming and co-creative thinking aloud? This is the Grassroots Spirituality Movement's third great challenge.

Other Projects

We heard several other ideas about possible common projects during our interviews. Some might be natural outgrowths of the dialogue processes we've discussed.

• **Spiritual "Houses of Life Development" (Spiritual HOLDs)**

> *"There are many people who would, if they had a year, spend more time in spiritual studies and less time trying to develop a career. . . . The religious vocation used to be respectable and admirable. I wonder how we could make it so again. Let's find a way to allow spirituality to mesh with the world, help create a class of 'non-traditional pioneers.'"*[5]

Speaking of retreats, Harvey Aaronson, a thirty-year practitioner of a variety of meditation programs, has attended retreats led by teachers from many, many paths. He notes that each retreat is typically attended exclusively by adepts of that one particular guru or lineage. Wouldn't it be wonderful, he wonders, if we were to create retreat centers whose participants come from many spiritual paths. He calls them "Spiritual Houses of Life Development" (Spiritual HOLDs). These centers might be made available — perhaps in exchange for work — for inexpensive weekend, week, month or longer periods. They could become sanctuaries for monks, laity or even families, and be *"open to exploring issues, contemplative traditions and a variety of*

paths."⁶ Such centers could also becomes centers of contemplative wisdom, and become schools for the dissemi-
nation of spiritual knowledge.

Such retreat centers might be HOLDs for not only meditation but also be centers for the kind of informal,
cross-traditional conversations we discussed above. Simply sharing meals and walks with people from other paths
could go far in opening both psychological, interpersonal
and spiritual windows. Thus these HOLDs would be one
answer to the movement's great challenges.

Aaronson believes that mature spiritual adepts would
need little guidance on their retreats at such a place. For
the less experienced, there might be some sort of direction,
perhaps by people like Harvey who is trained in teaching
one or a variety of contemplation techniques and spiritual
theories. Others might write, dance, compose or sculpt in
something like a spiritual artist's community. In this way,
the Grassroots Spirituality Movement would foster new
art, an approach that seems to threaten some conservative
religious leaders and politicians.

Speaking practically, our era may be particularly ripe
for this avenue. Many convents and monasteries are currently struggling for residents and income. As the numbers of people choosing to become (celibate) priests,
monks and nuns has dwindled, convents that used to
house many score of religious are now homes to half a
dozen aging residents. It might be possible for foundations or non profits to acquire some of these properties for
a reasonable price before they are sold off to developers.

• **A Spiritual Yellow Pages**

Several suggested the need for a "Spiritual Yellow Pages."
When someone moves to a new city, for example, it may
take many years for them to find good spiritual bookstores, decent coffee shops or group centers, or to identify
interesting people or a good spiritual support group. Furthermore, if someone travels to a new town for a week or

two, he or she might like to find a meditation space or group to "sit" with temporarily.

Thus there may be a need for some sort of directory of spiritual leaders and non-dogmatic groups. Such a directory might supply not only addresses and phone numbers, but perhaps be annotated with the days and hours of meditation, the teachers' specializations, the patterns or interests of the group discussion, etc.

In response to this need, The Forge Institute has recently put on its web site, www.TheForge.org, just a directory of its "Guild" members. These carefully screened spiritual leaders or teachers teach or lead a broad range of traditions. In signing onto the Forge's vision, they have each publicly stated that their path is not the only true way. In their Forge listing, each teacher has been invited to not only describe his or her work and programs, but also their ethical beliefs and commitments (no unimportant matter after so much chicanery amongst leaders of so many paths).

• **A "Life Consultant's" Seminary**

Many people suggested that some sort of Life Consultant's school could be of profound value. Such a seminary could train spiritual leaders in a variety of traditions, and train them in teaching a range of schools and development techniques.

Meditation teachers, spiritual directors, and other spiritual leaders have traditionally been trained in a single path, and in a more or less *ad hoc,* inconsistent way. Some have been given, under the tutelage of a particular school or guru, careful instruction in teaching meditation or in doing spiritual guidance. Others claim to have been given instruction by invisible spirit teachers, still others have built their teachings on a single insight or to have trained themselves. Some have had training in facilitation, psychotherapy, or marriage counseling, but not in traditional spiritual paths. Where can one go to learn of the full range of such tools, programs and techniques?

It seems possible, suggested many of our participants, that some reasonably coherent curriculum could be developed that might offer more systematic training in a wide variety of spiritual tools, techniques and philosophies. For example, one might learn Zen stories, TM techniques, Sufi dhikr, theories and techniques of clinical and group therapy and an array of spiritual philosophies.

Such a school might train not only group dialogue processes, but also Buddhist, Hindu and Sufi philosophies. Professors of spiritual direction and of clinical and group therapy could teach what they know, and so on.

We imagine such a school would be a cross between a graduate school program in comparative religions, a graduate school in clinical psychology, a non-denominational seminary, a facilitator's institute and a Zendo. Though spiritually oriented, it would be unlike a typical seminary in being explicitly trans-traditional. Unlike a graduate school in comparative religions, it would offer both academic and practical training in spirituality. Though it would teach clinicians, unlike a graduate school in psychology, it would include the mystery of the transcendent in its explorations of human nature. Unlike the traditional ashram, it would train people in a range of techniques, if they chose, and it would offer tools for offering additional modalities of human development. And of course its research functions would focus on consciousness and the nature of spiritual development.

A Life Consultant's Seminary might offer courses in trans-traditional dialogue, help participants become more sensitive to client's unspoken psychological material and assumptions, and instruction in mentoring people to help them find their own viewpoint and path.

Such a school could simultaneously satisfy several socio-spiritual needs:

- Train tomorrow's spiritual leaders, teachers, writers and spiritually oriented therapists.

- Offer training for both novice and experienced facilitators.

- Train novice and experienced meditation teachers in a wider variety of spiritual tools and techniques than is elsewhere available: i.e. other meditation techniques, how to facilitate spiritual groups in a range of ways, and perhaps basic clinical psychology.

- Advanced training — in one's own tradition and in others — for experienced leaders and adepts. While many spiritual leaders are clearly expert in their spiritual techniques or programs, they are generally much weaker when they try to teach the philosophical underpinnings of their or another's tradition.

- Offer training in organizational consulting, training for business leaders, and other institutional consultants.

- Become a home for research into the effects of meditation and other procedures, serve as a place to refine techniques, and possibly become the locus for the development of entirely new spiritual tools and techniques.

Such a school could, in effect, supply providers for our wider society's general spiritual needs. And they could become centers that develop and promote our general understanding of spirituality.

- **School for Youthful Seekers**

Another suggestion for a school comes from Dr. Mwalimu Imara. He envisions a small, full time academy for young people from a variety of socio-economic and ethnic backgrounds. In addition to the normal education, he imagines that this school would, on a non-sectarian basis, help young people learn a range of spiritual principles and traditions, as well as the sciences and arts.

Imara imagines that such a school might help its students learn to sense their own nervous system's responses, a self-referential "Bible of biology" if you will. The school might weave meditation, bio-feedback, Tai Chi and/or other tools into its curriculum to help children develop not only control over their minds, bodies and behavior, but also allow them to know spiritual happiness even in the middle of life's difficulties.

We tend to think of ourselves in non-biological ways, Imara continues. This school could help us get beyond this, to *"get to the central person who controls all these neurochemicals."* He imagines a kind of instruction in life technology, to learn what it is to become vulnerable, strong and open.[7] Obviously, says Imara, such a non-sectarian school would have to include tools from a variety of traditions to help young people develop.

• **Possible National & International Initiatives**

Several have suggested that by bringing varieties of spiritual leaders and practitioners into contact and dialogue, many interesting new projects become possible. A few ideas:

- • **Take your values to work day.** Several of our informants imagined a national incentive to encourage a day of discussions of workers' deeper values and aspirations. Modeled after the very successful "Take your Daughters to Work Day", people imagined yearly discussions of values in workplaces, schools, PTA's, and also in informal home groups.

- • **Meditation period in the work day.** If spiritual people in an organization militated for it, we could see an incentive to encourage businesses and workplaces to make room for a meditation/rest period during the workday. It might be optional, but choosing to use it would be generally regarded as respectable.

• **Retreat weeks in work package.** A similar incentive as the last, we might dream of a movement to encourage businesses to include retreats as part of their yearly or bi-yearly work package. For example, a business might offer, as part of its umbrella benefits package, a week at half-pay for someone to take a quiet life-contemplation retreat.

• **Decommercialization of funeral / burial procedures.** Funerals are generally run by businesses. We mourn our deceased in impersonal "funeral homes" where our beloved friends and family members are laid out in often enormously expensive coffins. They are buried in distant and expensive plots reserved for the purpose. Might it be possible to change the laws that protect the funeral industry, and allow the bereaved the choice to cremate their loved ones in their own favorite place, or bury them in their own way in the deceased's favorite place? Might we at least band together to re-think these practices?

• **Interdenominational Halls of Silence.** Several respondent suggested that if spiritual teachers cooperated, it might be possible for several groups to together construct a trans-traditional "hall of silence." There many groups might do their silent practices together. Such a place might be part of the trans-traditional spiritual community centers mentioned above, and offer day care facilities, meeting or class spaces, and generally be community centers for a local Grassroots Spirituality Community.

- **Buffalo Blizzard Time.** Arthur Waskow, a Jewish spiritual leader, suggested that part of the modern problem is rootlessness. We used to know our neighbors, and hang out together more in the back yards, he observes. But now we sit alone in our living rooms, watching more and more TV and AOL channels. Waskow noted how much people learn to appreciate each other during enforced vacation periods, such as during the famed blizzards in Buffalo, NY. He brainstorms that a number of grassroots spiritual groups might work for what he calls "Buffalo Blizzard Time" in which a town or a city comes to a halt. This of course is based on the Jewish Sabbath model.

"Say the Government declared that the whole of society were to shut down for a week, say the week of July 4. Except for emergencies, there would be no planes, TV, radio, etc. People would be encouraged to rest, get to know their neighbors, hold local festivals and concerts, etc."[8]

This would have the effect of encouraging people to build local roots, he believes, and establish a space for themselves.

- **Spiritual Media**. Several of our informants suggested that the spiritual world might create a national radio or TV show. It might have interviews with participants from every stripe, explore the nature of human growth, promote the practice of true dialogue, where people from various positions on an issue actually move their issue forward (as opposed to just disagreeing), and the like. Related to this: spiritual teachers might develop a series of "spiritual shorts" of a minute or so in length. Such "spiritual food for thought pieces might be distributed through Public Television, NPR, PRI or other media networks. These groups could also become resources for Bill Moyers and similar thoughtful producers.

• **Service projects.** Together spiritual groups small or large could form alliances to undertake projects like feeding the homeless that no single one of them could imagine undertaking. Groups might offer free or low cost workshops, spiritual counsel to the homeless, or arrange some collaborative efforts with a church or synagogue.

204 Grassroots Spirituality

Notes — Chapter X

[1]   Diana Whitney
[2]   Doug Kruschke
[3]   Jack Healey
[4]   Jack Healey
[5]   Tony Stern
[6]   Harvey Aronson
[7]   MI
[8]   Arthur Waskow

Epilogue

The Death of God,
The Birth of "It"

*For nearly two millennia, Christians had
believed that true freedom came from God.
Dante had proclaimed, "His will is our peace,"
and a thousand sermons had promised their lis-
teners that if they would only obey God's gentle
demands, they would attain eternal bliss. But
for two millennia the world had been grinding on
its inexorable way, crushing the bodies and the
minds of men and women, twisting them and
distorting their vision of the good. A new [model]
was needed.*

Charles van Doren [1]

In Chapter IV, we highlighted some of the causes of the
Grassroots Spirituality Movement. But I believe we left
out the broadest and most long-term cause of them all.
Our civilization has lost a plausible overarching theological model, and we desperately need one. It is this very
deep and long term human question I would like to
address in this chapter. For I think what is happening has
risen up is in part as an answer to a very long term human
quandry: What to do about "the Death of God?"

Much of Western life and religion had its conceptual
source in the medieval model. Medieval Christendom was
grounded in a far-reaching, integrated coherent life and

understanding of the universe, all "under" the wise leadership of God. So too, the Islamic world took its guidance from the Suras purportedly recording the word of Allah and the behavior and utterances of Muhammad. The medieval Christendom attempt, the attempt of Islam and of many traditional societies all over the world, was to pattern our lives on the God-given traditional social order, and play the "appropriate" role that God, and our caste or class had dictated. We were to think with traditional ways of thinking, worship with traditional chants (be they in Latin, Sanskrit, Hebrew or Arabic). We were to follow the clear cut ethical code that God had "given" and which was generally articulated and administered by our churchmen, priests, mullahs, monks or rabbis. The ideal was to live a traditionally sanctioned life, in which everything that one did was part of a wider and relatively coherent scheme, social network, and worldview. And always at the helm was believed to be the commanding presence of God, shaping and guiding it all through His Bible, Gita, Koran or Analects — under the guidance of "His" priestly classes.

This traditional and deeply hierarchical life was reflected and legitimated in many traditional theologies. Just as the serf looked up to the lord, the lord up to his prince, and the prince up to the king on his throne, so too all, even the king, looked up to and obeyed the commands of the divine King of Kings. We could respect our society's traditions, whatsoever they were, in part because they were understood to be divinely given. In other words, the hierarchical nature of society was modeled in and legitimated by the hierarchical nature of the divine.[2]

In such a traditional system — and it lives still in many lands — social pressures and dictates reign over individual freedom, choice and autonomy. Group-speak dominates individual will and individualized creativity. We see this in many traditional lands and in more traditional segments of our own modern societies.

In many ways this was a wonderful and uplifting model. It inspired in people a commitment to the ideals of their communities, a dedication to their belief systems, a life of loyalty and service to those higher in the hierarchy. It provided clear ethical guidance and an inspiring sense of virtue. Though for many it led to the misery of being dominated, for many if not most such God-centered systems brought a measure of safety, comfort and love — of our relations, of the sometimes admirable lords and ladies, of God and of our place in His well-organized kingdom.

But the traditional life began to unravel for a combination of reasons. We needn't explore them here in depth, but one could point to technological, demographic, educational, financial, political and other changes that led to its downfall in the West. As these coherent God-centered systems lost their sway over our souls, individuals began to understand themselves as equal to or *above* traditional ways of thinking. People en masse began to think for themselves. Once they did in the "Renaissance" and the "Enlightenment" and later, it was probably inevitable that many people would lose their infatuation with this all-encompassing model of a king-like God presiding in high judgment over all people. With more open thought and dynamic exploration, it was probably inevitable that traditional rituals would come for many to feel rote and meaningless. Since "He" had been so deeply associated with the traditional societal structures and thought patterns, this divine could not forever survive the cultural shifts that were undermining those very structures. In short the shift from fixed social role to entrepreneur shook the very foundations of that hierarchical God's throne.

In other words, it was probably inevitable that *that* God would die.

As our gods and the traditions they legitimated lost sway, human civilization has been searching for more workable models and more appropriate myths. During the last two centuries, and especially the last fifty years, we have searched through faddish new models: New Thought, Aquarian Ages, the Wisdom of the East, drug-induced insights, "channeled" prophesies, "new" Christianities, "renewed" Judaisms, and "New" Ages. What we have been searching for is a sense of the ultimate that might fit deeply with our mobile, individualistic, entrepreneurial, exploratory lives and minds. We are still in the middle of, or at the tail end of, this period of a thousand new religions: the Age of Searching.

I believe that the drugged and tie-died New Age, in other words, was a forerunner to today's saner and more mature answer, Grassroots Spirituality.

In it the ultimate, when it is identified, seems more like an "It" than a "He" or a "She." The "It" here is no longer some personalized and judging God-figure. In Grassroots Spirituality the ultimate is a much more integrated and immanent panentheistic presence. It is directly available to each and every mind and heart, no matter what social role or station we enter or where we move. Even those of us who lack a steady church community or even an intact nuclear family can remain in contact with "It." Because "It" is not conceived as person-like, It does not judge our actions, for It has no will and makes no judgments. It does include a vague sense of a life-direction which points us towards realizing more of our potential. But this is very different than a being who judges our behavior or dictates our actions. "It" is more like a hidden water table under us all that feeds and interconnects all of our wells than like a king high on his distant throne.

Yet Grassroots Spirituality adamantly refuses to ossify this panentheistic ultimate with some fixed catechism. In fact, a key stress in Grassroots Spirituality is to remain ever-open to spiritual inquiry. For spirituality is understood as a fluid and in part not-strictly-rational journey of self transformation and self-reflection. Spirituality within the grassroots now centers on this process: open not-strictly-rational self-reflection, self-inquiry, heart-felt conversations, and a sincere and ongoing questioning about what is real and who we are in relation to our larger self and to each other.[3] It holds and defends the product of these explorations with little exclusivity. And it values both private exploration and open group processes.

In this way, Grassroots Spirituality may have discovered a plausible and satisfying answer to the very old problem of the Death of God — that is, to the death of the hierarchically-grounded trust in fixity, absolutism and group-think. For when religiosity *centers* on a process of open self-exploration, spiritual inquiry and mutual examination, it offers a way towards wisdom that does not require us to impale our lives on the twin poles of certain beliefs and fixed behaviors.

Tradition-centered religions that legitimated the fixed and unchanging social lives of their era tended towards a fixity of belief and behavior.

To Grassroots Spirituality that very stuckness became one of the presenting problems. It responded with a cornucopia of not-strictly-rational tools and techniques to break through such adamantine stuckness. Not only does it provide tools to help thaw ancient frozen attitudes, it offers new directions and insights about "It," life and the universe.

These Grassroots processes of spiritual exploration and the use of the not-strictly-rational also answer to the problem of rituals that seem dead, and to many seem to be rote. Meditation, small groups, mutual exploration, an attitude of unknowing, the sense of exploring "at the edge of what we know," unpredictable and indescribable mystical experiences — whatever else might be said of them, none are rote or predictable.

As it is practiced today, spirituality substitutes if you will a discipline of *process* — always insisting on openness, self- exploration and group dynamics — for a discipline of *belief.* It does not require that one buy into any particular belief or language system. In fact, it refuses to land in any dogma. Rather its members are determined to remain open to exploring their lives, their habits of thought, and the full range of languages, paths and rituals.

One side point. Grassroots Spirituality does not avoid all theorizing: thousands of books have emerged from its ranks. Its theology seems to fit like a key in a lock with our modern worldview. The doctrine of a panentheistic ultimate tends to fit more elegantly with the worldview offered by modern physics — of a single underlying energy within all matter and all space — than does the model of a distant and creator God.

Grassroots Spirituality is by no means without its own inherent flaws, of course. Primarily it conceals a built in tendency towards entropy and anarchy. It often seems as if anyone's explorations can go anywhere, say anything, or even do anything. But does absolutely "anything" go? Is there nothing (beyond the illegal) that we could all agree is absolutely *wrong*? Does nothing at all count as "out of bounds?" Who is to say, and how are they to say it?

Similarly, if "everyone" is a priest, who will organize, lead, or orchestrate the necessary group processes? What is a leader in this profoundly egalitarian context?

Third, there is a tendency to reject any repetitive rituals as "rote" or "formulaic." But if we reject them all, then from where might come the rituals that we can treasure and to which we can go in a time of need? From where will come those ritual moments that allow us to join and connect with one another in that non verbal way that has been so important to humanity for millennia? Rituals are important, if only to give us tools and images to think with, grounds on which we can stand. Yet, given our multiplicity of traditions and sacred tongues, what might such a grassroots ritual possibly look like?

Spiritual Christians and Jews, as we saw, are attempting to preserve their beloved rituals, even while rethinking and rewriting some of them. In this they are attempting to solve just this problem. But Jewish leaders or Unitarian Ministers are of a *single* tradition. We have not yet learned how to develop satisfying rituals that would work for folks of all traditions.

Forth, if everything is fluid and relative, how are we to find stability? What is it that will hold spiritual groups and our larger society together? Will merely having a "core agenda" or a "core intention" be enough?

Finally, under the natural desire to transcend them, spiritual people exhibit, according to many psychologists we spoke with, a dangerous tendency to deny or avoid their messier, more negative or complex feelings.[4] This often leads to a kind of pseudo-enlightenment, an outward pretending to not be bothered by life's troubles. This generally collapses in disappointment and/or anger under the hard knocks of reality and marriage.

Yet these problems do not seem insuperable. We believe that with work, thought, and continued awareness of these issues, the Grassroots Spirituality Movement offers a profoundly optimistic answer to the problems which it has arisen in part to answer. It offers the possibility of real connections, a sense of deeper purpose to life, and a way to heal both our bodies and our souls. It offers a solidity of being rarely available in other ways.

The "It" towards which we grow may offer, in short, a powerful and compelling solution to the hole in our universe and our hearts left by the Death of God.

It is worth beginning.

212 Grassroots Spirituality

Notes — Epilogue

[1]   Charles van Doren, *A History of Knowledge* (NY: Ballentine Books, 1991), p. 241. For much of this last section, I am indebted to van Doren's trenchant analysis of the problem of the medieval mindset.

[2]   For the substance of this paragraph, I am indebted to Rosha Forman.

[3]   Tony Stern, paraphrased.

[4]   Something Jung first noticed, calling it the "mana" personality.

The Forge Institute

In Chapter IX we reported that many participants of the Grassroots Spirituality Movement feel alone and devoid of support.

> "*I sometimes feel I'm the only one doing this work,*" said one.[1]

> "*I wish we could create community,*" mourned another.[2]

> "*I think that there is a deep spiritual need for a real sense of community.*"[3]

In addition, we saw, because the movement lacks a larger infra-structure, its members often feel relatively powerless. There is no natural community or natural means of networking. As a result, their efforts seem to be a drop in the bucket, their effects painfully small.

Since conducting our interviews, we at The Forge Institute have responded to these requests by developing the kind of communities, networks and programs for which we heard people calling:

> "*Let's create a space where organic spiritual values can emerge. We'll bring in more and more people for this process of dialogue and mutual growth. Little by little, we expand our groups to include more. We'll dialogue and taste each other's worldview and experiences and grow together. I think there needs to be a space, a community. I*"

don't mean a new religion. I'm imagining a space where values like diversity and growth and openness can be cultivated."[4]

"[Let's] communicate with people from other traditions to help us break down the barriers. We could see what we share. For example is meditation something that we share? Is Quaker silence different from my silence? Are there common practices? This could be an exploration with others. And it would be good for this to happen on an ongoing basis."[5]

"The idea here is to create a community among those who are leading the spiritual groups, spiritual peer groups."[6]

Such communities, we heard, should be non dogmatic, open to a range of practices, and based on common spiritual ground. People told us of their longings for ongoing, healthy communities and links among them across the nation and world.

So The Forge Institute has responded by beginning just such communities. We have fostered them among three relatively distinct constituencies: (1) **The Forge Guild**. This, our first program, is for spiritual leaders and teachers, the good hearted folks who are explicitly helping others develop spiritually. (2) **The Forge Public Wing**. We are fostering communities of people who are serious about their spiritual life and are interested in being with and learning from people on a variety of paths. (3) **The Forge College and University Program.** We have begun both for-credit and extra curricular college courses. These programs are for students and eventually faculty and staff who want to explore their spiritual life but don't want to be told what path they "should" take or how to think or act.

First, a word on The Forge Institute itself.

What is The Forge Institute?

The Forge is a unique educational organization. It is, to my knowledge, the first spiritual home and support system that is led by spiritual leaders and teachers and people from a broad range of spiritual paths, styles and persuasions. It is not a church, for it has no dogma or beliefs of its own. Rather it seeks to provide containers and opportunities for people who hold to its basic vision to gather and to foster what we call "spiritual wisdom" in themselves and the larger world.

Simply stated, the Forge's purpose is to "contribute to a renaissance of spiritual wisdom in our pluralistic world." It is our way of working to address problems not in a short term way, but in a real and long term manner. I think, and others in the Forge think, that the real basis of the world's problems is not the politicians or the economy, but egocentricity and the attachment to our ethnic and religious divisions. So we seek to address both issues by bringing people from all paths and traditions together, to help them learn to help each other let go of those egos and divisions in a way that both celebrates their differences and at the same time transcends them, and to help them stretch their lives towards the spiritual ground together. Our hope is to help more and more people and institutions consciously strive to live a fully integrated life and to help to foster it in each other. That's the royal way to real and long term solutions, in my view.

The Forge's vision centers on what we call "spiritual wisdom." In many ways, this term constellates what we heard in our interviews, but is a bit more focused.

We didn't invent the phrase "spiritual wisdom." People use it in lots of ways. But we've defined it carefully, and in a special way. First, we mean by this term a way of being alive, a way of holding the world or carrying one's life. It points to the kind of moment in which we're connecting with ourselves and/or others in a particularly deep and open fashion. The times that we're *really* present, and deliciously open.

"Spiritual wisdom" points to the feeling or experience of being in an open yet deep exploration with fellow seekers from many paths. But it's also the attitude that takes all of life and even its problems as an opportunity of growth, as a place for wonder and curiosity and expansion. It's marked by a curiousity and an interest in life and in other paths, without trying to convert or be converted. And it's a life whose most precious quality is the deep sense of connection to the divine, to the spirit, and the sense of being of a piece with that panentheistic one.

If we're to tease out what goes into this general gestalt, we might say it has three essential but somewhat independent components.

1. Being fully open to an infinite spiritual awareness — however we name or conceive of it — amidst our joys and sorrows, our commonalities and our differences.

2. Consciously acknowledging that there are many valid spiritual paths, even while remaining centered in our own.

3. Being committed to ongoing growth toward fullness and freedom, with open minds and light hearts, in every domain of life.

Since we developed this term in part out of the conversations behind this book, it is no surprise that many of our interviewees have told us that they live by just the general attitude pointed to by this term. This is no doubt the reason that many of them have joined our young network, for it intentionally describes the very commitments they described to us.

In order to help foster this approach in participants and in the world, the Forge's vision calls for the development of "spiritual wisdom" in oneself and in each other. It has a lovely way of expressing Gandhi's famous dictum that "you must be the change you want to see in the world:" we must live these values in "the I, the We, and the World." By these three domains we mean:

- **The I:** Deepening our own spiritual wisdom and more consistently expressing it in all areas of our lives.
- **The We:** Forming a diverse, co-creative community that exemplifies and fosters spiritual wisdom in all its interactions.
- **The World:** Enhancing the ability of each of us to aid the spiritual development of others, and working collectively to foster the growth of spiritual wisdom in society.

Now, to manifest these three missions, The Forge has begun three programs.

1. The Forge Guild

This is the world's first professional association for transtraditionally oriented spiritual leaders, teachers, writers, scholars and others who are helping to bring spirituality to others. These highly talented spiritual leaders, teachers and writers in the US, Canada and Europe are Jewish and Christian clergy, spiritually oriented psychotherapists, health practitioners, authors, researchers and circuit speakers. It has chapters around the United States and Canada. We ask Guild members to nominate only the most inspiring spiritual leaders or teachers they know who celebrate that there are many paths and who are interested in helping others foster a more spiritual society. We actively seek diversity in religion, race, orientation and spiritual pathway. It takes two nominations to be invited into the Guild.

All Guild activities stress going beyond tolerance and respect to actually experiencing common spiritual ground and helping each other grow as both spiritual people and spiritual professionals. Guild members seek to help each other bring spirituality more effectively to those we each serve even though our approaches may differ. But please be clear that this work is not replacing anyone's tradition, but rather is designed to strengthen each participant's path by helping each deepen his or her awareness of the infinite, whatever it is called.

Membership in the Guild offers access to chapters, regional retreats, international conferences, newsletter, website, email discussion forum, and more. Its teams or committees are developing an ethical program, a one on one "soul friend" system, a range of workshops, chapter development, public programming, a "public voice" for spirituality and other programs. Each is designed to further some aspect of the vision.

Forge Guild members are:

- Creating an infrastructure for the vast Grassroots Spirituality Movement that has never before existed.

- Finding and spiritually engaging with other spiritual leaders and teachers from a variety of paths, thus deepening their lives and growing spiritually in ways that any single tradition might not make available.

- Serving as professional consultants and advisors for one another, improving their professional skills and improving their abilities to serve their particular constituents.

- Helping each other increase their audiences, through both mutual support, publicity in each others' programs, and through the Forge's own activities.

- Developing a coherent public voice that stands for a path-transcending spirituality.

- Helping restore the public image of spiritual leaders and teachers by developing a clear and strong *ethical* program.

- Joining forces and developing common projects. Guild members have helped each other in educational, interfaith, health related and other programs.

- Developing common efforts to bring spiritual wisdom to the seeking public and to society's institutions.

2. The Forge Public Wing

The Forge Institute has begun a program for seekers of all denominations and paths in Westchester county, just North of New York City. Though it does not have a physical space of its own, we think of it as creating something like a trans-traditional "community center" for diverse seekers. Two things happen in this young but growing community:

(1) *Regular community-wide programs.* These monthly gatherings might involve in-depth meditations, facilitated dialogues, rituals from a range of paths or some other programs designed to foster spiritual and psychological growth in our diverse setting. In addition to some practice or instruction, these gatherings offer opportunities to explore participants' most meaningful life experiences, heartfelt struggles or life-commitments. And there are no dogmatic answers to these deep and personal questions. Instead the idea is to simply help participants explore their *own* answers in their *own* way.

(2) *Spiritual programs from every major tradition.* Because The Forge Guild is comprised of such diverse teachers as Buddhist and Jewish clergy, Hindu meditation teachers,

Christian chaplains, spiritual psychologists and other diverse spiritual leaders and teachers, it can make available a rich cornucopia of long-term offerings from our various traditions or paths: classes, practices, rituals and other programs from the various pathways.

Why are people coming? We have learned that our participants tend to be people who:

- Desire spiritual growth but aren't fully satisfied with their current options,

- Sense that there is much to be learned with and from people from other paths, but have no natural way to find them,

- Long for a supportive community that cuts across traditional lines,

- Are curious to learn from a range of teachers and paths, but have no systematic way to find excellent ones.

Our participants are people who have often felt alone in their spiritual quests. They've been asking, "where can I go to deepen my own life and to find others interested in these questions who won't try to sell me their answers?" They've often wondered where they might go to find reliable resources to continue their psychological and spiritual development. They've wondered where they might go to learn how to develop healthy patterns of communication.

The Forge offers all this and more. It asks only that participants do not try to convert each other.

3. The Forge in Colleges and Universities

As the Forge has begun to develop programs for the public, it has also begun to ask how can we in the spirituality community foster greater wisdom and connection on college and university campuses? Following the guidance we heard from the interviews that form the research behind this book, we've been asking how might we create the kind of space that makes it safe for individuals to reach towards the depths together, and again without imposing any particular dogma or beliefs? In short how might we create an educational model for waking up?

The Forge has developed a unique kind of college program designed to encourage participants to explore their common spiritual depths while exploring their very real diversities. It focuses on the students' life direction and commitments, and fosters the exploration of diversity while exploring students' common spiritual depths.

The Forge is beginning to offer for college credit a one-semester course in colleges and universities around the US and Canada. Facilitated by Forge Guild members, it is a rich program oriented around the wisdom of the traditions and paths and a series of facilitated self and group explorations into the spiritual life.

The class is entitled "Spiritual Diversity in Contemporary Society: Theory and Practice" That last word, "practice," is the key, for the 36 hour program is oriented around actively developing wisdom among our students. The "theory" in the title refers to the theoretical elements of the course that helps students think critically about that development process. It focuses on self-reflection, for spiritual wisdom can emerge, we believe, only when knowledge is combined with experience and reflection on it. So the program invites in wonder, ceaseless questioning, and makes room for the students' exploration of the ineffable. Its lectures, by renowned spiritual leaders, and its facilitated discussions are all designed to offer content for and to make it safe for students and others to share about their own depth experiences, and to hold a space for the mystery of the spirit. It teaches the practice of real listening and self-disclosure, and in the process invites participants into the privilege of authentic dialogue about unanswerable questions.

In all these ways, The Forge Institute is attempting to realize the spiritual dreams and aspirations that we heard in our interviews.

For more information, please call The Forge Institute: (914) 478 7802 or write *Admin@TheForge.org*.

Notes — Afterword

[1]   RKC
[2]   Stuart Smithers
[3]   MT
[4]   Tony Stern
[5]   Arthur Waskow
[6]   Stuart Smithers

INDEX

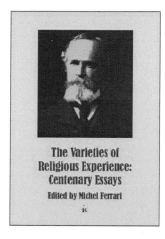

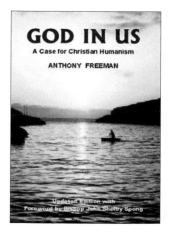

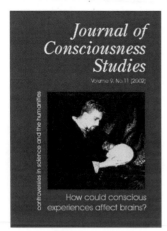
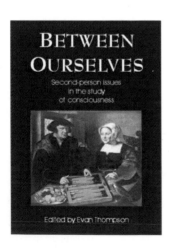